STRIVING FOR REDEMPTION

MEN FOR HONOR

Edited by
DORTELL WILLIAMS

East Oakland Times, LLC

Contents

ARISTOTLE

"The virtue of justice consists in moderation, as regulated by wisdom."

This book is dedicated to the innumerable victims and survivors of crime. We, the participants of the Men For Honor, individually and collectively, apologize for the wrongs we have done. We apologize for the harm we have caused to you, our communities, and society as a whole. We are truly sorry, and are now trying to transform our maladaptive thinking, make amends and help others to do so.

Foreword

The Men For Honor Present:
Striving For Redemption

We push, we struggle, and we strive. What all the contributors to this book are striving for is personal development and rehabilitation. The Progressive Programming Facility, named officially in 2007 by the California Department of Corrections and Rehabilitation, under Governor Arnold Schwarzenegger, offers these aims and more. Through the PPF, we have succeeded in creating a path toward personal reformation. The program was actually implemented in the winter of 2000, when prisoner Kenneth E. Hartman, with the support of many other reform-minded prisoners, such as Charles "Chuck" Russ, proposed a plan to allow these prisoners the opportunity to volunteer to create a positive maximum-security facility.

Then Warden Earnie Roe, and a priest named Thomas White, supported the vision with some 600 prisoners of all races, representing a wide array of communities. The main tenet of the facility, called the Honor Yard, was that it was voluntary. Participants most apt for the program were those who sought personal change in their lives, those who wanted to shake the senseless violence that brought them to prison in the first place, and miss the damaging pressure and trauma of prison politics.

The proposal established that the facility be dedicated to those who wished to program in a positive way. At minimum, the program required that an applicant have three years of consecutive, trouble-free programming. Participants are required to relinquish all gang and hate-group ties, and submit to random drug testing. Each participant, once cleared through screening, must submit a one-year plan for self-help and personal development.

Participants with skills were commissioned to compose a curriculum for their skill-set and then teach it to a class of approximately thirty of their peers. So the sick help cure the sick, an evidence-based approach that has proven successful enough for recommendation by licensed behaviorists. Prisoners skilled in, say, painting, creative writing, or math, teach their peers these skills. An inmate instructor who teaches Spanish one cycle, may be a student under the tutelage of another prisoner who is versed in victimology in the next cycle.

The California prison system allows prisoners to create inmate-led groups called Inmate Leisure Time Activity groups, or ILTAGs. It is through these groups that various activities for the Honor Yard are formed. Some groups focus on helping at-risk kids, such as C.R.O.P. (Convicts Reaching Out to People), or supporting personal development, such as the Men For Honor. Others focus on Music, such as

M.U.S.I.C. (Men Utilizing Sounds to Incorporate Collaboration) or dog training, such as PAWS for Life. There are a multitude of groups, offering a bevy of programs.

Within the first three years, the Honor Yard had proven itself an indisputable success. Richard Faucett of the *Los Angeles Times* reported that weapons infractions, violence and threatening behavior all but disappeared – by over 80% in each category. Additionally, drug-related offenses fell by 43% (and in the editor's opinion, this is the area where professional help would likely be most effective given the chemical/physiological nature of drug addiction). Given the success that these numbers represent, it was challenging for even the program's detractors to disparage it.

However, as a result of statewide overcrowding, the Honor Yard's mission was changed to a general reception facility in the early 2006. Public support from dignitaries such as State Senator Gloria Romero helped pressure CDCR to prioritize the program's survival. Upon its re-implementation, support for the Honor Yard gained such momentum that a senate bill, the "Honor Yard Bill," was introduced on its behalf. Established by the State Public Safety Commission, the bill passed remarkably, with bi-partisan support. Many onlookers were amazed that despite the cantankerous relationship between the Democrats and Republicans, both parties agreed with a yard full of convicts, and overwhelmingly passed the bill. The Bill, officially registered as S.B. 299, was simple. Its aim was to compel CDCR to establish an "Honor Yard" on every maximum-medium-security facility in the state. It was a common-sense, evidence-based bill. The reason for this action was that, after six successful years, CDCR headquarters refused to even acknowledging the program, much less support it. Unfortunately, Governor Arnold Schwarzenegger refused to endorse S.B. 299, instead adding a signing statement explaining that CDCR could simply implement such programs on its own.

Six years later, in 2014, CDCR designated seven maximum-medium-security facilities as Enhanced Programming Facilities. This is a good start; however, as recent as the fall of 2015, CDCR was being criticized for the unbridled violence in its institutions, and a homicide rate that measures twice the national average.

In 2007, the program was finally recognized by CDCR, and officially renamed the Progressive Programming Facility. The motto of the PPF is, "Breaking through the past, progressing towards a better future." The purpose of the PPF is to create a peaceful, programming environment that allows, and even promotes, personal growth, rehabilitation and instill pro-social values within its participants.

As you will witness by the pages in this book, the difference in a programming facility verses a non-programming facility is the overall disposition of the collective population. It all boils down to perspective. Not much different from the individuals who commit crimes in society, and then come to prison. It's about perspective, tweak the attitude, add a little hope and, or, incentive and the individuals who make up the overall population become self-motivated to better themselves. Another difference is the cost. In the Honor Yard's first year of existence some $200,000 was saved in taxpayer monies. As it turns out, violence is expensive: overtime, emergency transport, lockdowns, higher-grade equipment to quell the violence, and structural damage.

As you will read, for the majority of us, violence and the ensuring lockdowns are a distraction from the goal or rehabilitation. It is difficult, if not impossible, to concentrate on cognitive improvement when one's mind is stuck on watching his back for literal survival. It is challenging to find like-minded individuals in a cesspool of racial hatred, rebellion, gratuitous violence and self-hate.

The PPF continues to grow and flourish. The PPF continues to save taxpayers bundles of tax-payer money; remember, most of the unique programs offered on the PPF are peer-to-peer, meaning there is little to no cost for priceless, life-changing results.

In 2013 nearly ten life-term prisoners earned parole from the PPF, an unprecedented number in such a short span. The State Board of Parole Hearings specifically cited many of the peer-taught programs as a basis for influencing favorable decisions to those who went before them. For those of us barred from review by the BPH, due to sentences of life without the possibility of parole, self-development translates to more peace and harmony. Peace and harmony is derived from new coping skills, and the satisfaction of positively contributing to the lives of others.

The ILTAG H.E.A.R.T. (Helping Everyone Attain Real Transformation) is a prime example of such pro-social work. H.E.A.R.T. helps and supports indigent prisoners earn their G.E.D.s and eventually college degrees. H.E.A.R.T., the parent group of F.O.L.C.C. (For Our Local Community Charities). F.O.L.C.C. crochets clothing for local charities, such as St. Jude Research Hospital. H.E.A.R.T. also facilitates the Lionheart Foundation's "Houses of Healing" program, which helps prisoners confront and deal with past traumas, and negative events in their lives that may be rooted in their criminality.

There is also L.E.F. (Lifer's Education Fund), a 501(c) (3) non-profit that provides scholarships to prisoners who have demonstrated their ability to succeed at higher collegiate levels. Then there's Healing Through Arts, which promotes outside organizations such as Wounded Warriors and Gold Star Mothers. The Veteran's Group does the same, while encouraging and actively supporting the vets participating on the PPF.

Prisoners of the PPF also provide many health-oriented courses that are taught by certified peer-instructors of the Inmate Peer Education Program. These prisoners concentrate on the prevention of, or treatment of, infectious diseases such as hepatitis-C, HIV/AIDS and others. The healthier we are in here, the healthier we are when returned to society.

Of course, CDCR offers a number of mandated education/vocational programs. Academic education is mandated up to ninth-grade level, but prisoners can volunteer to earn their General Equivalency Diplomas. These programs are available through the Adult Basic Education program. CDCR also offers English as a second language, and some vocational programs, depending on the prison. These trades can range from welding to cabinet-making to plumbing, but they are very limited in availability. In fact, less than 2% of the entire prison budget is dedicated to such programs. The higher the level of security, the less opportunities. It is primarily for this reason that we create our own programs. As you will read, the waiting lists for these ILTAGs and other self-help opportunities is never exhausted.

Contributors of this book will share how yoga, graphic arts, music theory, sign language, and business classes have helped them to grow and discover themselves. They will describe how film studies, English as a second language, Spanish and peer-taught ethnic courses have helped change their thinking, change their course, and changed their lives.

These groups, and many more that have risen and fallen

during the existence of this positive program, all strive to give back to society in some way. Many participants – who really get it – vow to never hurt another human being again, by touch or tongue. Others give back to society by means of direct donations, fundraisers, and, or cooperative partnerships with outside organizations. Helping Hands makes it its mission to donate to outside organizations for themes such as cancer, childrens' causes and religious organizations. The Progressive Arts Program (PAP), formerly known as Artist Serving Humanity, donated $50,000 to outside organizations, such as Toys for Tots, before it was converted to PAP.

It is the educational and artistic opportunities that give the PPF its success. In contrast, as you will read, the intolerance of even minor slights or perceived disrespect, such as stepping on someone's shoes, or mindlessly staring in one's direction, is quickly dismissed. PPF prisoners strive to look beyond such trivialities; we exercise empathy and compassion, and if nothing else, we duel it out in civil debate. Respect is liberally given and exchanged on the PPF, to both prisoners and staff. Our collective mindset on the PPF, where reverse peer pressure is used to persuade new guys to "get with the program," is to tolerate those irritating habits, and idiosyncrasies that seem to pull the very fiber at each individual nerve.

That said, prison, even the PPF, is filled with men who come from dysfunctional families, pronounced character flaws and faulty thinking. Participants get into scuffles on the handball court every now and then. Drugs and alcohol, even cellphones are found on the PPF. We're a work in progress. But in measure, the PPF is more safe and successful than any of its alternatives, and that's why we think you should read about it.

Sources:

California State Prison – Los Angeles County, Facility-A Progressive Programming Facility Orientation Guide, 2013

California State Prison – Los Angeles County, Men For Honor Pamphlet, 2015

Faucet, Richard, "Honor Program Success," *Los Angeles Times*, 2003

Honor Comes Hard: Writing From the California Prison System's Honor Yard, (Edited by Luis Rodriquez and Lucinda Thomas, Tia Chucha Press, Los Angeles, CA 2009) pp.6-8

Thompson, Dan "Overcrowding Linked to Deaths (AP), *San Jose Mercury News*, February 18, 2015, p.B5

Too Cruel, Not Unusual Enough: An Anthology Published Through The Other Death Penalty Project, (Edited By Kenneth E. Hartman with John Purugganan and Robert C. Chan, associate editors, 2003) P. 217

Wood, Daniel B., *The Christian Science Monitor*, November 11, 2012, pp. 44, 45

SUSANNE K. LANGER

"Philosophizing is the process of making sense out of experience."

Men For Honor (M.F.H.)
Preparation for life

The purpose of Men For Honor is to effect rehabilitation through programs that utilize ownership; constructive problem solving; academic curriculum, vocational training; real world skills, the exercise of positive social norms, and giving back to the community.

Men For Honor restores inmates as stakeholders in their own lives.

A prison is a prison, from the outside looking in, they're all the same. Yet, like those distant, deep-water mollusks; the uniqueness of each of their precious pearly treasures aren't revealed until one takes a closer look inside.

— Dortell Williams

Men for Honor: From Then til Now

Men For Honor took roots in 2002, two years after the approval of the Honor Program. The ILTAG originated as a health and fitness group called the Self-Development Program. As time passed, and management of the group changed, so did its name and focus. A new mission statement was adopted, "... to promote a productive and peaceful environment of learning, by utilizing our mutual skills to teach one another and build self-worth; life skills, and gain a collective appreciation of one another."

The most radical changes occurred in 2005 with its flagship class, Critical Thinking. This class was Men For Honor's sole class until 2007, when Dortell Williams was asked to instruct Creative Writing. A Film Studies class was then added by a staff librarian that everyone called Mr. D. He had a heavy Greek accent, and would teach the class on Saturdays, during his off hours. Mr. D had a master's degree in film studies. Albert Izuel enhanced the Men For Honor learning experience with the insightful instruction of a business class.

By this time, Men For Honor had earned enough respect to offer a one-day orientation seminar every six months, informing new arrivals what academic and programming options were offered on the PPF. In approximately 2009, the Men For Honor began collaborating with other prisoners outside of the group, to present one-day seminars on Nutrition, HIV/AIDS prevention, and courses on communicable diseases.

Typically, we place sign-up sheets on the walls of each of the four housing units for interested prisoners to sign up. The Men For Honor executive body then chooses names based on race, proximity to release (or a Board of Parole Hearing date), and history of attendance/attitude in previous classes. The population on the PPF has almost always been predominantly African-American, so just about every prisoner from the other ethnicities are given priority in order to give racial balance to the classes.

There are almost always more people signed up for a class than there is room to accommodate them. The classes run from one to two hours, depending on class availability, and the curriculum offered, and endure for ten to twelve weeks per cycle. Just about every class requires thirty hours of homework, per class. The best writers are typically avid readers, so the Creative Writing class presented the need for a more literary-focused library. As a result, the Men For Honor Library was created. The Men For Honor Library houses some seventy-five books: literary poetic, instructional and academic, as well as screenplays.

As the classes continued to be filled to capacity (27-30 students per class), more types of Men For Honor classes were added in an effort to meet the demand. In 2012, New Choices, Different Directions was added to the Men For

Honor cycle as an answer to gang violence and group criminality. Many prisoners who have never participated in gang activity take the course to mentor troubled youth.

In 2013, Sharing of Language was added to support the various ethnic groups who could use help in improving their communication skills, as well as learning various self-help techniques in their own language. Workforce Development was subsequently added to help the many prisoners who have never been challenged by the experience of completing a job application, much less an employment interview. Personal Development followed, to expose long-term prisoners acculturated into the toxic environment of prison culture, or the 'hood, to mainstream etiquette and culture.

It was easy for us to relate to, and understand, that many prisoners come from dysfunctional families, and neglected neighborhoods, where they were labeled "at-risk," and yet no one ever intervened in their desperate, misguided lives. Many prisoners are graduates of nothing more than the rough school of hard knocks, discouraged and dissuaded from reaching their dreams or potential. Men For Honor believes that the classes it offers helps prisoners catch up to the mainstream, gain what they originally missed, or were deprived of, and offers them, if nothing more, the foundation for a second chance.

It is this ideal of second chances, and a fervent belief in generating hope, that Men For Honor began offering cognitive behavioral therapy classes such as Victim Sensitivity, Helping Youth Under Stand Their Harm, the lifer Therapy class, and Creative/Reflective Writing. Each of these classes focuses on emotional intelligence and impulse control, handling suppression, and anger management. They also concentrate on personal trauma, and recognizing traits of trauma in others, while tapping into empathy, and cycles of aggression and violence. Finally, as if poetry itself was our guide, the Men For Honor completed a full 360 by re-enlisting Critical Thinking to its cycle.

As with all ILTAGs, Men For Honor is self-sufficient, and funds itself through fund-raising campaigns. These campaigns, usually in the form of food sales to the prison population, encourages cohesiveness toward a common goal, reveal the rewards of collective partnering, and give the men an opportunity to think beyond themselves. In most cases, most of the fundraising proceeds are donated to a charity. The vast majority of prisoners involved appreciate any chance to give back and make amends.

Over the years, Men For Honor has made donations to such organizations as the Los Angeles Children's Hospital, the non-profit, Los Angeles-based Continuing the Dream Foundation, as well as homeless shelters, re-entry organizations that assist parolees, and women's shelters. To date, Men For Honor has donated over $15,000 to various charities.

Beginning in January 2014, Men For Honor began a separate philanthropic effort called Caring For Others. This project encourages its participants to collectively donate quarterly, apart from the bi-annual fund-raising campaigns. At the beginning of each quarter, the Men For Honor executive body votes on three local charities with similar objectives, for example, children's organizations and cancer foundations. After this process, three like organizations are presented to all of the Men For Honor participants for a final, blind vote. Once a charity is selected, a voluntary collection is offered once a month in each class. Following a three-month collection period, the proceeds are forwarded to the selected charity. A staff sponsor controls the collections, verifies the totals received, and releases sees the donation through.

Much of Men For Honor's success is due to active partnership with outside organizations such as the New Beginning Outreach Foundation, in Lancaster, California, which aims to help parolees successfully re-enter society and live a crime-free life. Men For Honor also partners with the Los Angeles-based Partnership for Re-Entry Program (PREP), which offers parolees a network of transitional housing, along with life skills and job support. On behalf of PREP, Men For Honor also facilitates life-skill lessons to the PPF population to give substance to otherwise bland warehousing, and actually attempts to replace the criminal mindset. The courses cover everything from domestic violence to anger management.

As of September of 2013, Men For Honor has partnered with Prison Letters 4 Our Struggling Youth. Prison Letters ... strives to reach troubled youth by facilitating admonishment and guidance letters from men who have been there and done that. Some 1,500 prisoners throughout California's prisons write these important letters. Men For Honor continues to expand, aiming to have a meaningful, positive and expansive impact on both sides of the wall. We hope that you enjoy our presentation.

JOHN LUTHER

"Build character piece by piece: by thought, choice, courage & determination."

Beginnings

BY JOEL N. AGUILAR

The morning had been somber but warm, with a heaviness that would mark me for many years to come. I sat on the porch of Big Rascal's house as three other homies talked about Dreamer's death. Dreamer was murdered by an enemy of our neighborhood and it was the first time – as a gang member—I had mourned for a homie. It was the summer of 1988, the beginning of my life as a gang banger.

Dreamer had been walking on the sidewalk with Cecy. Bandit retold the events "The homie looked in love; he and Cecy were holding hands, walking on Elendale Street when a red truck pulled up and blasted the homie." The image forced my eyes shut the and air out of me. I remembered Dreamer's smile and the way it widened symmetrically with his eyes. Dreamer was also fifteen and a Salvadorian. The short period I knew him seemed like a life time, as if we'd known one another our entire lives.

I had a grim epiphany that day; that I could be the next

Dreamer. I let go of the girl crushes and other teenage activities and took on the complete mindset of survival. I had reached my limit.

There were questions settled and decisions made in the chambers of my heart that morning, and though Doper and Bronco had been killed months before, Dreamer's death felt closely personal.

Drive-by shootings ripped through our neighborhood, one after another. The days were dangerous, the nights murderous. Toyota Celicas and Chevy Regals were cars to watch out for, especially if they drove through at a crawls pace and the front lights were turned off. My neighborhood became a place where children no longer played peacefully on the streets and the recreation parks that were meant for them became gang hangouts and drug spots.

For my sake, I felt I had no other option but to assume this crazy role. So at sixteen, I got the initials of my neighborhood − sort of drawing the line on my body—tattooed on my left triceps. It was my statement to my 'hood' and the enemies of my hood. Pedee, who we called Loui, was with me that night and praised my decision with "that looks bad ass!" his compliment was validation that I had done the right thing. Twenty years of Harpy's history lay across my back arm, marking not only my allegiance, but the curse that seemed to follow each one of us as members.

I was proud of that tattoo but scared of what my parents would think and say. At the same time, my school grades were plummeting. They had been since my second semester at Robert Frost Junior High. Truth was, the curriculum was too advanced and I could not keep up. Everything about that school seemed to be above my expectations: from the beautiful location of Granada Hills, to the delicious bagels served at brunch, to the plush carpet that floored the classrooms and hallways. Everything about foster was so unfamiliar. I felt out of place. I could not understand why I had such a hard time learning.

As my grades declined, my street rep ascended. There was something about being in a gang that enchanted me, while everything else made no sense.

By the middle of eighth grade, I was transferred to join John Adams Junior High to back up some of my homies against rivals. The older homies would gather after school, and together we would beat and chase down anyone who was from a rival gang. Other times we were the ones getting chased and beaten. It was a cat and dog chase that escalated in violence until it just became too dangerous to attend classes.

From there I was transferred to Foshay Junior High, located at the border of my neighborhood and where some of my other homies attended. Although the gang violence was not as intense at Foshay, back in my neighborhood the drive-bys were getting worse. On one occasion I had come over to Hoover Park and the homie Porkey sat at the bench while two other homies stood aside with their heads hanging low. "The homie Lazy is dead" Porky intoned in a low voice.

In that second, I knew exactly how Porky felt. Lazy was his Dreamer. They had known each other before joining the 'hood. Their parents were from the state of Mexico and they both had brothers who were also friends. For their sake, for Dreamers' sake, I wanted revenge. Lazy was my age and I'd had it with being a sitting duck.

In 1990, I would be entrusted to the Los Angeles juvenile hall, fighting a murder I did not commit. It was in Los Padrinos where I relieved my fears. Through a collect call I heard the words I feared to hear. "They killed Loui bro, Pedee is dead" said my brother. In an instant my vision was blurred with tears and I could hear my brothers' shaky voice and how hard he'd taken Pedee's death. Loui had been like a big brother to me and he was the cousin of my best friend, Alex Reyna. Whenever there was a shot heard around the 'hood, Louie would go out to find us and make sure we were alright.

In the sixteen years I had lived on this earth, Loui was the last person I imagined ever being killed. "Bro," I said "how'd he die?" there was a pause, "He and Poppies were chased down in a car, and they crashed but were able to run and hide. Poppies said that as he hid under a car, Loui stood beside a fire fighter at the fire station, the one next to USC (University of Southern California). But a dude jumped out in a ski mask and ran up and blasted him" I took a deep breath. "Who did this?" I demanded. I could feel the grief creep on me, but I clinched my teeth as hard as I could and caught myself.

Louie's death took a while to accept, but when reality came, a piece of my sanity had left. How I wished I was back at my neighborhood but maybe I would have been killed too. I was enraged. I was so confused about what I was brought to this world for. Shortly after that episode, I found myself in the hole for rushing someone who accused my 'hood of killing his uncle. His mistake was not striking first.

Perhaps at that moment, being locked up in solitary for a couple of weeks was good for me. But as I put all my energy into push-ups, jumping jacks, and shadow boxing as an escape, I received a letter informing me that my homie Snake had been killed. I was re-living death over and over again.

Dead, another one. "Ah, damn it!" I whispered, as my fingers released the letter and my body throbbed with intense emotion. I remembered Dreamer; I remembered Loui, and now Snake. "How could all of this happen while I was away? I asked myself.

The cell became colder and lonelier. I remembered my bedroom, my small twin-sized bed, and I wished and wished I was home.

The days turned to years, or so It felt, as the longing to be with my homies grew stronger. When I slept, I dreamed: a procession of homies and family were lowering my walnut-colored casket into the bland earth. When I woke, there I was in a concrete casket of sorts, and there only were thoughts of the homies' faces I would never, ever see again.

The juvenile court found me unfit to be tried as a minor and I found myself headed toward Central Juvenile Hall. Central was the place I would encounter my most hated enemies. Those who allegedly were to blame for the deaths of my closest homies. As soon as I stepped into the unit, I was approached by an enemy who threatened, "We'll get down later." Which meant that at the first opportunity we would go head up, one on one. I waited about a week; I was anxious by then. My arms were loose, my mind was set and I was ready. When feeding was over and the staff was out of sight, I bolted out of my cell and into my enemy's cell. As soon as he saw me, we struck at each other's faces. That scenario repeated itself four more times, with four other enemies.

Soon after my last fight, I had again received bad news. This time Danny, Grumpy and Gordo had been chased down and popped inside Danny's car as they crashed while attempting to flea a hail of bullets. Gordo was Danny's nephew and was only thirteen-years-old. I knew then that things would never be the same in my neighborhood.

In October of 1990, I was released from juvenile hall. As I figured, everything had changed. The young vibrant faces of my homies' had hardened and aged. Their disposition carried the hardships of the 'hood. While I was locked away, punching enemies in their faces, the homies were dodging bullets and burying other homies.

The streets were quiet and gloomy under my returning feet. Within no time, the target of death had returned to my back. Not long after my release, during a solemn walk, I felt a sudden pain sting at my left thigh, the force dropped me to my knees. I could hear bullets whizzing above my head and hitting objects near me. When the shots stopped, I got up and all of the homeboys seemed to have disappeared. I limped toward the open street and caught my homies' car peeling off. "Hold on!" I shouted and jumped through the passenger window. I thrusted and twisted, grasping at the backseat. "Take me to the hospital," I yelled. My wounds were superficial.

That night my homies and I decided to pay a visit on our enemies. As we chased them toward their back yard, one of them opened fire and shot me on the left hip. For a split second I thought that night was my last. This was the miracle that my mother had always prayed for when she locked herself in the bathroom and lit her *veladora* (candlestick).

The neighborhood grew more dangerous; the neighborhood streets became death zones, while back streets remained secret safe routes. Any vehicle with two heads inside were immediately considered possible enemies. Without the agreed upon headlight blink, a friendly sign among ourselves, the approaching car would have been met with at least two pistol barrels up their noses.

The street lights were shot out and the hangout was made pitch black. We did everything possible to increase our chances of survival. The mission was to stay alive, and beating the enemy on the draw could mean one more night a mother slept knowing her boy is home and safe.

I remember jumping back yards, running past barking dogs and following night cats through dumpster alleys to get home safe. Sometimes I would sprint a block, duck under a car, watch and listen ... then sprint to the next block until I got home safely.

On one night in particular, the 'hood had been hot,' enemies had shot at one of our hangouts. The homies were on full alert when half a dozen shots rung about two blocks away. Screeching down the block we noticed the homie's car swerving recklessly. Then suddenly, the vehicle stopped at our location. The homie steps out and starts yelling, "They shot Gumby!"

Gumby was slumped on the back seat, motionless. He couldn't he helped. But another homie jumped in the car and drove him to the hospital, in vain. In less than one year, from my release from juvenile hall, I buried Blacky, Sammy, Shy Boy, Shorty, Crow and Sleepy.

That was my life on the outside. My entry into prison wasn't much different, at least in regards to environment. While I've managed to straighten up quite a bit, the environments of various institutions did nothing to help my personal growth or reformation. Not until I was transferred to the Honor Yard two years ago.

It was here, at the Honor Yard where I was able to flourish

and really grow in positive ways. Since my arrival here I have benefited from classes such as Friends Outside conflict resolution, which offers a number of ways to solve conflicts. The class is structured as a group of us, all with the same problems, shared experiences, sharing various ways we failed or succeeded in resolving conflict. I've learned to accept the meat in these group settings and throw out the fat. The instructor, a small, patient woman with an engaging personality, leads with professional approaches to conflict resolution. I completed the class feeling like I accomplished something important and with a new set of skills to help me succeed.

I was introduced to the Men For Honor Group through their Film Studies class. It was taught by the librarian, who volunteered his time to teach the class. I remember he had a PH.D. in something, but was also very knowledgeable in the history of film making, including foreign films. He gave a lot of homework and was liable to call on you during class, so we had to pay attention. It was a discipline, Later I took the MFH Creative Writing class and was able to hone my skills a little more through that experience. It was in that class that I was offered a position on the executive body, and that experience in leadership will always reward me. From there I was invited by the group to co-instruct beginner Spanish, which also had its rewards. The payment of self-satisfaction, self-esteem and the opportunity to prove myself was priceless. As well as the rewards of just paying it forward and benefiting from the experience.

I also benefitted from Paving Way, which is a class offered by an organization by the same name that offers in-depth instruction social norms, family relationships and life skills. I gained skills and outlooks I will never forget from that class.

As a practicing Christian, Malachi Dads was another class

that helped to foster positive approaches to life. This organization sends volunteers into instruct on parenting from a biblical perspective. Several instructors come in and we break off into small groups of, say four, and discuss the week's topics according to the Bible. Topics such as fatherhood, or patience or love are discussed. It was a well spent three months of my time.

I am now working in the main kitchen and do not have quite as much time to take so many classes. But I still enroll in at least one correspondence college course each semester and I take classes here and there.

Since I was arrested as a juvenile, and modern science has proven that juvenile brains are structured less adequately for planning and decision making than adults, I am more grateful than ever for this experience and the healing and coping techniques I have learned to deal with the traumatic childhood I had. I'm sure my neighbors in society will be just as grateful. I'll make sure of that.

Joel Aguilar was just a few weeks shy of his eighteenth birthday when he entered the prison system. Now, in his early forties, Joel is a confident speaker, a positive influence, a challenge to anyone who says, "I can't."

In his spare time, Joel is an avid reader, a prolific writer and an opponent to watch for on the soccer field. He talks college classes to make up for lost time, and will tell you in a heartbeat that it's all about the Trojans (USC).

He follows the Bible and leads the lost – even while successfully finding his own way. Joel Aguilar was eventually released as a result of the Supreme Court cases, *Miller v. Alabama*, prohibiting the sentencing of juveniles to life without the possibility of parole.

"Character is the sum and total of a person's choices."

P.B. Fitzwater

Home of the Happy Pen's Club

BY DOUG PORTER

A room, is a room, is a room, and for the life of me, I can't find anything about this place to boast about. Sometimes the room is unlocked, while we're using, but most of the time it is locked—like most rooms in a prison.

In a place like this each room is different, but every room has a lock. And for the most part, every room we're in is locked by protocol. This particular room offers a chalkboard, three long, white-surfaced tables and any number of chairs, depending on the purpose of those using the room at the time.

I'll bet you no one has ever painted a picture of this room, yet a lot of pictures have been painted in this room. If someone did paint a picture of this room it wouldn't be much of a picture because there just isn't much to it. If I ever leave this place, I'm certainly not going to remember this room.

On the other hand, most Tuesday afternoons this room receives a group of talented, diversified young men that share a potpourri of thoughts, ideas and visions forever recorded on paper. For me, it's one of the rare times I get to somewhat leave prison – if not in body, in mind.

At times I'm impressed, even entertained. The men often make me smile, and occasionally laugh. From time to time I'll see one of these young men out on the yard or in one of the housing units. I give them a polite, compassionate look and then become saddened. Prison is such a waste.

However, this is the place we must be for now. At age sixty-two, I'm a little older than most. They call me "Coach," because I used to coach wrestling. So mentoring comes easy for me, as well as teaching.

My introduction describes the room we use for the Men For Honor Creative Writing class. This class, and the relaxed atmosphere I alluded to, are kind of unique to the California prison system. Here, not only is mentoring easier, but also doing time in a peaceful way. The last institution I was at had many alarms, like this one. The difference here is that most of them are either false or on another facility that doesn't have the positive programming we have here on the Progressive Programming Facility, previously known as the Honor yard.

Even at my age, I have benefitted greatly from the self-help direction of this yard. Not long ago, I graduated from the Malachi Men course. It was a twelve-week course brought by Godly men, volunteers, who help teach young men how to be responsible family men; guidance I believe this generation seriously needs. Not only was the class educational, but it was fun, which helped the men relax and open up in the group.

I also had the pleasure of instructing the Men For Honor Spanish class, along with Brother Hilario Arroyo, who is actually from Mexico. I learned the language by conducting missionary work in Mexico years ago. I am good at teaching the dynamics of the language, and Hilario is an expert at accent and pronunciation. As you might imagine, Spanish is a plus in California, whether in or out of prison. So the men appreciate the class a lot.

The pleasure in teaching classes like this, and even the Men For Honor parenting class, which I also instruct, is that these men line up to enroll. I've never seen such a thirst for personal growth like I've seen here. But then, I've never been at a place where opportunities for self-help were so open.

There are many men who sign up for parenting, and do not have children. When I ask them why they sign up, they tell me that they can use the skills with younger brothers, nephews and even youngsters here on the yard – they come in younger than ever these days. I tell them "Great!" The farther we can take this, the better, is my thinking.

As a Christian, this place is a haven for what we call "the harvest." Here, a majority of the guy's hearts are already open. They have shed the masks and hard looks used for survival at other places and are ready for change. Here, the men are more authentic and approachable, because there's nothing to prove here. The culture is about self-betterment. Here, achievement is applauded.

I still genuinely believe that in many cases prison is a waste, but at least here on the PPF the men can actually build something positive during their stay. That's not only good for them, that's good for their families, and for society.

Who could ask for more?

Doug Porter is a respected, gray-haired elder on the yard who is known for endearingly calling everyone "Son." He is an apt father figure, perfect for instructing the MFH parenting class.

Wise with biblical wisdom and application, Doug is a peace-maker, a guide, a leader.

A former wrestler who's still got a move or two, and a San Francisco Giants fan to the fullest. That's Doug, a proud papa and friend to all.

"More men are good by training than by nature."

Unknown

Saving Grace: What Society Doesn't Know about the PPF

BY LIL' Q

Trapped in a fictitious world of make believe Corrections, a beacon of hope and inspiration shines, brightly cutting through the prevalent haze of doom and gloom.

Allow me to introduce myself. My name is Lil'Q, a prisoner at the State Prison in Los Angeles County (CSP-LAC). Who knew that one day I would be singing the praises of anything having to do with the California Department of Corrections and Rehabilitation? Yet, the Progressive Programming Facility deserves such praise. But before I go any further with this story, let me give you a brief description of who I am and the bumpy road I had to travel to receive this blessing.

I was born and raised in the cutthroat streets of the San Francisco/Oakland Bay Area, in California. I came to prison at the age of nineteen. To date I have spent a consecutive total of thirty-three years of my life as a state prisoner. But not even the mean streets of my upbringing could prepare me for the savage, manufactured bizzaro world of prison. Not by any stretch of the imagination am I what I would consider an angel, yet standing all of 5'7" in stature, and weighing in at 175 pounds, I came to prison for first—and second—degree murder. I received a concurrent term of fifteen and twenty-five years to life.

Young and impetuous, I was a wild child who would spend my formative years fighting for my life, as well as my manhood. (In the early years of the California prison system there was always someone lurking about looking to make some younger or a weaker prisoner his wife.) Yeah, though I walk through the valley of the shadow of death, I will fear no evil. For I was the meanest, baddest so and so the Bay Area had spawned—or so I thought. But prison is the school of hard knocks. And I had to learn a whole new game, as well as its vicious rules and as such, my life would plunge deeper still into a world void of both night and day. In prison time is only a figment of one's imagination. Right became wrong and wrong became the natural order of things, and as a result, I adopted a more fatalistic persona. I had become so indoctrinated to the norms and standards of prison life that I had begun to lose my humanity. I eventually bought into the unique ideology of prison and its warped social expectations.

For example, there are subtle but distinct differences between being an inmate and being a convict. While most prisoners can be cutthroat, or at least a little shady, inmates are generally your run of the mill drug abusers, dealers or petty thieves who just happened to have been caught. Inmates are here today, gone tomorrow, and for the most part they take on that frame of mind. They take little, if anything, in prison serious. They have no real stake in what goes on in the long term. Convicts (the lifers) are typically the exact opposite in thinking. Convicts are typically brooding and pragmatic. They carry a surface calm that belies the calculating turmoil that is the life of the lifer. Every action, every conversation, is a measured step toward the ultimate goal of survival—minute by minute, through each day. The goal is to survive without losing your mind.

California law mandates that its lifer population meet a very stringent criteria to be remotely considered a viable candidate for parole. Among these criteria are educational achievements, vocational training, participation in self-help and group therapy. Lifers are also expected to remain disciplinary-free, and maintain a positive rapport with staff, which is shown through laudatory documentation. All of this in an environment that is contrary to these goals. Lifers are expected to do the near impossible. To quote a phrase made famous by the old-school funk band, Parliament-Funkadelic, lifers are expected to "dance under water and not get wet."

The challenge of successfully programming without incident for decades at a time is made more difficult in these budget-restrained days of cuts and slashes to programs that were designed to at least balance the chaotic environment with personal growth and rehabilitation. Prisons, as I've known them, have always been violent places. The violence leads to lockdowns and the lockdowns result in mass stagnation. Keep in mind that lockdowns can last from a few weeks to a few years, depending on the situation, emergency or disturbance.

A war zone is a war zone, and I was trained to take my tour of duty seriously. Remember, at the end of the day, prison is about survival, otherwise nothing else matters.

I was on the front lines of some of northern California's most notorious battle grounds. I survived in the fog of violence with a determination to just keep moving forward, putting one foot in front of the other—without getting tripped up by others or my environment.

I didn't realize that I had become a member of the emotional walking dead. To me, and so many others, nothing mattered, not freedom or life. I took on the frame of mind that when in Rome, do as the Romans do. And that's exactly what I did. I made many, many more trips to the hole. I was a gladiator in mind and body, but the senselessness of it all also began to weigh on me. At some point you realize that something must change. I came to realize that it had to be the man in the mirror.

Borrowing from biblical wisdom: I Corinthians 13:11 says, "When I was a child, I spoke as a child; I thought like a child; I reasoned like a child. But when I became a man, I put childish ways behind me." I came to see my environment and my involvement in it, for what it was. I began to shift my focus. The desire to become free from the surrounding forces driving me developed its own drive. Unfortunately, old habits die hard. Besides, where could I go to separate myself from prison life when everywhere I went was the same? Little did I know, but God had other plans for me.

While still stuck in those war zones, I got into yet another one of those inevitable, violent wrecks. It was the same ole song; the same ride I'd ridden on so many times before. And once again, I found myself in the hole for the crime of battery on another inmate with a weapon.

I had always wanted to write a book, I just never got around to it; too distracted watching my back, trying to survive. Typically, the hole has a lot of activity going on; conversations; fishing from cell to cell. (One guy makes a line out of whatever he can find, anchors it with something heavy, like a rubber slipper, and throws it down the tier to another cell to trade magazines, food or whatever. In the hole people tend to do anything to keep from going stir crazy.)

With not much activity in the hole at CSP-LAC, I took to writing. My first book, "Town Business...Money, Redemption, Revenge" was born in the hole. Surprisingly, writing this book would lead me to a world I never knew existed. Excited and desiring to share my accomplishment, I found myself enrolled in the Men For Honor Creative Writing class after I was released from the hole. Here was a group of men who weren't very different from me. They wanted something different, something above the typical prison existence.

These guys didn't just want it, they had actually succeeded in stepping away from the rank and file of prison politics. They had become their own men, and were encouraging others to do the same while leading the way. Here at CSP-LAC your sentence didn't matter, Convict, Lifer, Inmate, whatever your frame of mind, this place had something to offer.

I was utterly amazed to see so many men—most of whom are serving life sentences—doing everything they could to effect change within themselves *and* their environment. Inspired, I began enrolling in every class the Men For Honor group offered that I thought might help me re-build myself. I wanted to address various character flaws, strengthen my self-esteem and confront my anger, the underlying cause of my criminal behavior.

The Victim Sensitivity class helped me address my self-esteem and anger issues. I also learned what empathy is and how to possess it and transfer it to others. It is as simple as putting yourself in the shoes of other, especially victims of crime. But to prevent crime, which is even better, I learned to humanize people, as opposed to viewing them as a ticket or free ride for my selfish needs.

I learned job preparation and resume writing in the MFH Work Force Development class. These classes are designed to build leaders out of damaged men who have made up their minds to make a positive impression on those who might follow. Eventually, I was chosen as an instructor for the Lifer class, teaching other lifers how to be the men they were meant to be, in spite of their sentences.

I also got involved in a youth-mentoring organization called, "Walking the Yard," which is designed to have older prisoners 'walk the yard' with youthful prisoners and school them on the right way to do time. While mentoring is an act that is supposed to benefit others, it has its own personal rewards as well. Youth today can be challenging and mentally sparring with them, trying to get them to see your point is funny at times, but always thrilling.

Soon I will be graduating from the Channel Islands Bible and Seminary College with an associate of arts in Bible Studies. I have also earned a certificate in addictions counseling, and another certificate in family counseling through Channel Islands.

To someone from the outside looking in, these classes may seem small and insignificant. But to someone who has only known cruelty and been intimate with despair, these classes and our accomplishments mean the world. The Progressive Programming Facility has helped me to rediscover my humanity, and as a result, I will never again be the same man I was when I was arrested.

Lil Q is the author of *Town Business: Money, Redemption, Revenge*. Available on amazon.com. He is currently working on his second urban novel, *Fyre and Brimstone*. Lil Q is an avid sports fan, who also enjoys stimulating conversations and old-school R&B from the '70s and '80s.

JOHN MILTON

"The childhood shows the man, as mornings shows the day."

Living in Rage and Chaos

BY DONALD MOSS

My life in prison started June 21, 1981. I was nineteen years of age, and convicted of second-degree, gang-related murder. I will be the first to admit that my life before prison was a ball of confusion. Violence, destruction, and chaos ruled my life. My lifestyle didn't stop at the prison gate either. In fact, I doubled down on my activities. I had no reason to care, not for other people, nor myself. If you weren't a part of my cause, I had no regard for your cause. Period!

I quickly became deeply embedded in the prison culture of violence. I spent a lot of time in administrative segregation (the hole), and an even greater amount of time in the more restrictive security housing unit (the hole under the hole). I had an attitude and my resolution for any conflict was violence. And despite these extreme places of deprivation and punishment, I wasn't at all deterred from remaining true to the cause for which I represented. In fact, I just pushed back even harder.

Racism wasn't part of my daily view on the outside. But as a child, I had some dramatic racist experiences with white folk that were etched into my being. Still, I wasn't a racist. I just adopted the view, as I would say, to only be racist toward people that were racist toward me. That was until 1982, in San Quentin prison, when the Mexicans and whites teamed up to attack us blacks. That was my first race riot. It was a welcome to prison that completely changed my way of thinking. That experience also made me realize how serious prison life is. From that time I determined within myself to be ready at all times. That was the reality of prison life that I was confronted early on.

Living the lifestyle of the streets, and the culture of prison, hardened me, it hardened my soul, numbed my emotions. My focus was so narrow to my cause that I saw nothing else. As time went on, I sunk deeper into the swamp of prison life. I was knee deep in disruptive activities. Whether directly or indirectly, my fingertips were on it. I was so engrossed in me, my cause and my surroundings that I shut down communication with family and some of my dearest friends – because they weren't like-minded. I sought encouragement, a pat on the back, from my peers, for doing the right thing in the world I was now entrenched in. This world was full of fighting, stabbings and whatever destruction could be made. Upholding the unwritten rules and being defiant of authority and mainstream thinking was my mission.

My placement in prison was in some of California's darkest institutions. I found myself doing hard time, filling up my file with one disciplinary infraction after another. Then, one day, I woke up from my darkness. I realized that I was living a chaotic and lonely life, and I was on the fast track to an early grave in prison. I had to change my life. I quickly came to the realization that I couldn't change my environment, so I needed to work hard to change myself, in spite of my environment. I wanted to start by changing the way I think. I was never really a vocal person, I believed in less talk, more action, my voice was violence. I knew that negative viewpoint needed to change to a more positive one.

One day a counselor asked me if I wanted to go to Lancaster's Progressive Programming Facility. I was about to self-destruct and say "no" because of the "soft" perception I had of this facility, and the caliber of prisoners there. But after thinking about it, and removing my pride, I agreed. I haven't looked back.

When I arrived, someone I knew from a previous institution approached me, and we talked about the program. He told me about all of the classes offered, and asked me if I wanted to participate in any of them. It was at this point that I was told about the Men For Honor Group.

I signed up for their Lifer class, the Victim Sensitivity class and the Criminal and Gang Members Anonymous (New Choices, Different Directions) class. The New Choices class opened my eyes to the fact that I was loyal to a fault to a group of people who had abandoned me in my greatest time of need. I was growing up in the gang, trust was ingrained in me. But as time went on, and especially when I came to prison, I learned that worthiness was an illusion. Gang membership has an expiration date that costs your loyalty, most likely your freedom and possibly your life.

New Choices also helped me focus on the root causes of my joining a gang. I began to understand that I was living a dysfunctional lifestyle, and the importance of acknowledging my dysfunction. It was like the secret is out of the bag and now I can publicly share my defect. They say the surest way to a cure is to first acknowledge that you're sick. Now, with the help of these classes, I am actively working toward personal growth and change.

I remember giving a homie a pat on the back when he represented our gang according to our expectations. That was the culture of the environment. Here on the PPF, we give one another confirmation (a positive pat on the back) for self-betterment. We applaud each other in group study for opening up and admitting past wrongs, for confronting the shame and admitting the pain.

The Victim Sensitivity class helped me to realize the damage I had done, and to accept responsibility for my destructive past. VSA helped me focus on my victims and the harm I inflicted on indirect victims, like the community as a whole. I gained empathy for the pain and suffering I put them through as a result of my narrow, selfish thinking. And the class also helped me realize that I could change myself from this dysfunctional person, to a whole and contributing person.

This is my story of how I began my inner change thanks to the PPF and the Men For Honor Group. It is my hope and aim to evolve into a better person, not only for myself, but for the people in my life who are dear to me, and the community as a whole.

Donald Moss is a fifty-two-year-old man who has been incarcerated for the past thirty-four years. Donald began his hellish stint in the belly of the beast as a self-destructive youngster on a mission to destroy himself and as many others as he could, both mentally and physically. He was doomed by his own negative beliefs and activities.

For the last fifteen years he has grown tremendously. He became aware of his destructive beliefs and his issues: anger, faulty beliefs and negative responses.

Donald now encourages others, dissuades faulty thinking and mentors youth on the facility. He likes to exercise, read self-help and other books and write as a craft.

He is a confident, thoughtful and courteous man, mature and gracious. He reaches out to other troubled souls in hopes of restoring them to humanity. Donald is now on the right path and has tamed that beast—at least the one within himself.

EUNICE SHRIVER

"Use adversity for a purpose."

Growing Leads to Change

BY KORY DARTY

The waves of the world are impossible to drown people that are built to last. Good roots will always withstand the storms of life. The answers to any harvest lies in every person.

After chastening my flesh, I put myself in position to utilize my tree of gifts. I went through life's experiences with study and observation. I found purpose in my pain, my trials have become my testimony. I am living witness that hard work with honesty, dedication, and insight does pay off.

I have discovered that my ultimate strength is in the midst of strife and challenges. I have always wanted to be more than street smart, so I have established a different set of motives and principles to live by. Self-reflection helped me return to my gentle traits. I am aware of the magnitude and impact of my old rebellious way of living. When temptation resurfaces, taking healthy and positive actions over and over again strengthens my will, and nurtures the seeds I've planted. I have established a more solid foundation, and I continue to grow.

Self-assessment has rippled through my life with meaningful and lasting rehabilitative effects. Men For Honor self-help classes, creative options outside self-help courses, and Janie Hodges' Relationship Building Workshop/Paving the Way Foundation, has helped me identify the root of my behavior problems, and has helped me discern ways to deal with the symptoms. When the going gets rough, the resources I've obtained in Creative Conflict Resolutions has helped me a lot.

Partnership For Re-entry Program, life skills, and self-development modules have been good food for my journey. It's a daily duty because I do these courses in my cell.

Self-examination and personal inventory is very important, and keeps me alert. When I am in the wrong, I address my faults with honesty. If others are in the wrong, I proceed with caution and I show empathy. I know and understand the people in prison come from many different backgrounds and have different character traits. No matter the situation, I'm responsible for my actions, and my own peace in prison. Some officers try to assassinate my focus by saying they know I'm breaking prison rules, but my way of life, and my prison file, speak for themselves.

I have done the work to avoid volatile situations. Thanks to God, the one that gave me the wisdom to articulate the knowledge I've obtained on A- Yard, Lancaster State Prison. The Holy Spirit is my teacher, and I'm still learning. Effective prayer and meditation leads me.

I, Kory Darty, am proof that rehabilitation is possible for inmates that don't even have a date to go home. Instead of blaming others, acting out and letting prison break me, I give energy only to things with value, and carry myself as a productive citizen of society.

Today, I am a product of my education and inner authenticity. It wasn't easy to be the man I've become, but it does feel good.

"Philosophizing is the process of making sense out of experience."

Susan K. Langer

Chasing Rehabilitation

BY LARRY MAY

Years of exposure to racial aggression and daily violence were the source of my nightmares, waking up in sweat and fear. All of this after I left the "cushy" San Mateo County Jail in 2006.

I was headed to prison, San Quentin. Just the name San Quentin struck fear within me, and it lived up to its notorious name. I think the place should be sold. The mosquitoes, mice, and ants were a constant problem. Plus, there were plumbing problems all the time; mainly leaks. It was disgusting.

Walking the corridors reminded me of how ancient the place was. The cells were the worst. They were small, very small – fifty-square feet – for two of us. It might have been the conditions that caused so much hate: overcrowded, cold, and lots of ugly.

I have never seen such hateful looks until I went to SQ. Looks that sent shivers down my spine. I spent months there in the Reception Center. The showers were every other day. Along with the intimidating looks. Inmates stood and watched at the entrance of the showers on each side. A guard was above us on the catwalk with a gun in his hand at all times.

There were ten showerheads, and each race had a certain number. It was like high school all over again. Some men stared at other men's privates. Nothing could have been more uncomfortable. The shy, and scared, washed themselves in the sink in their cells.

We had yard twice a week. The all-cement area was also divided by race. There was no mixing allowed. I grew up in the racially balanced Bay Area, in San Francisco. So this was all a total shock to me.

Fights led to blood, blood led to running guards, running guards led to suffocating tear gas and the burn of pepper spray. It was a scene that was a daily occurrence. Each race has a person in charge of their race. One of the first nights there, the white leader jumped into my cell to "talk" to my cellmate and I. He said, "For whites its mandatory yard. If you don't participate you will be stabbed." I couldn't believe my ears. He was dead serious! It made me tremble. I was being forced to join ranks, and take orders from men I wanted nothing to do with. They were trying to turn me into a racist, something I'd never been before.

Out of nowhere, a guard came through, making his rounds. He saw three of us in the cell. I thought we were in big trouble. I thought I was going to be handcuffed and counseled. But the shot-caller told the guard that we were busy and to come back in fifteen minutes. And the guard did! That's when I realized the severity of the situation.

On the walk to the mess-hall, it was almost guaranteed that an incident would happen. Guards would throw inmates up against the wall, sometimes for no reason. If it wasn't the guards messing with inmates, it was inmates fighting inmates. I can't count the amount of times my dinner got an extra dose of seasoning: pepper spray.

No programs at all were offered at the reception center. Not even chapel services. Finally, I was transferred to Pelican Bay. This prison was newer, the cells were larger and the place was cleaner. But as I learned real fast, the prison politics were the same. I lived near some white supremacists. To keep the peace with them every month when I went to the store, I bought them hot cocoa.

My college background made me a candidate to be a tutor. My job was to help other inmates get their General Equivalency Diplomas. This was very rewarding for me, and some of the inmates appreciated it. My job made me well known around the yard. I earned respect by helping other inmates, not stabbing them. Few programs were offered, except education and religious services. My pastime was running laps, running in prison gave me something productive to do; it kept me out of trouble and kept me in shape. My running in Pelican Bay would frequently be interrupted by some kind of skirmish. The alarms would sound. We would be ordered to "get down." But not to just sit down, but to lay down flat on the ground with our faces looking into the dirt. An army of guards would respond to break it up. They would close in, and toss concussion grenades in the general area. Once, a grenade rolled close to me, it exploded and white powder went everywhere. My ears were ringing for hours after that.

On another occasion, while at Pelican Bay, a loose handball rolled over into the Asian area. I went to retrieve it and almost caused a riot. Each race must stay in their own area, no exceptions!

When the shot-callers at Pelican Bay tried to dictate my

program, I paid to move out of there, but the cell I had, had to remain a white cell according to the skinheads. The skinheads also forbid whites from accepting unwanted food off of a black's tray. It was like being in prison inside a prison.

It seemed as much as I tried to avoid trouble, it was always near. I loved going to the yard and running, but even such a harmless desire seemed to result in some type of drama. One of the most heartbreaking scenes I witnessed was after this guy had just finished shopping. A group of other whites approached him, kind of surrounded him, and after a brief exchange the guys started snatching his bags from him. The bags ripped apart and as his canteen fell, they started grabbing items and running in every direction. He just stood there in shock, to this day that scene saddens me.

After four and a half years my nightmare at Pelican Bay ended. Only to resume at the State Prison of Corcoran. It wasn't by choice. The racial segregation at Corcoran was pretty much a mirror to Pelican Bay. Likewise with the petty prison politics. Again, there were few programs offered, and the religious activities were cancelled constantly. Every race had their claimed areas and every race covered their own if one of theirs had to use the toilet to take a leak.

The typical race riots, the fighting, the destructive cell searches that always came next were enough for me to grow tired after just two years I ended up staying in my cell more than I went outside. I felt like I had to walk on eggshells just to survive. I didn't want to be jaded, I definitely wasn't going to be a racist, and I didn't want to turn into a recluse. I prayed for something, anything to change.

During my annual committee hearing I was given the option of transferring. Since I had no disciplinary infractions my custody level had been dropped from maximum-security to medium, and everything was in my favor. I was offered a transfer to Lancaster's Progressive Programming Facility. I chose to go there because of all the good things I had heard about it. When others heard about my transfer they called me a "sellout". On the other hand since I'm not into drugs, alcohol, or any other vices, Lancaster was right up my alley.

But when I arrived at the PPF, my troubles weren't over. I was told there was no room for me. I was sent to the hole. (They told me I wasn't being punished for anything, they just didn't have any beds yet. Yet, with no yard, no phone calls, and no dayroom activities it sure felt like I was being punished. I had never been to the hole before and don't ever want to go back.

The good thing was that I was never bothered by having to share cramped space in the hole with a cellmate. Still, it was a horrifying experience. The hole was filled with men who had lost all hope, or who were just down right evil. It was a hodgepodge of misfits. Men on suicide watch, men who dressed as best they could to appear as women, and men who spent their days and nights constantly masturbating. The guard would cover their cells with sheets or big yellow towels. And I was right smack in the middle of this madhouse.

After seven long days, and eight restless nights, I was finally headed to the PPF. On the yard I ran into old acquaintances from Corcoran, and Pelican Bay. These were the few guys I could relate to even back then. These guys were like me, they just wanted to do their time as peacefully and productively as possible. They just wanted to help others if they could, and be left alone. Older, mature men who had either been there and done that, or who had enough sense from the beginning to just program and make the best of it. I would guess that the average age here is fifty. The younger men here are more open to listen, but there are always some who only learn by constantly bumping their heads against the walls.

The first think I asked was, where are the racial lines drawn? Who has what areas and which side of the dayroom is for what race? To my disbelief, I was told that I could go wherever I wanted. Unheard of in California prisons! There are no racial divisions here. The tables, the phones, everything is open. The only area where the inmates divide themselves is in the cells, and that's not by force, but more for cultural likeness, music, and et cetera.

I was leery at first. When I jogged around the track I was on constant watch for anything odd. But it was the same scene each and every day, mixed races playing sports. Not race verse race, but mixed teams, as if race didn't exist. As I relaxed, I noticed that the atmosphere is peaceful. There is no racial or other tension here.

A first for me!

Another first was seeing the Bible study group, consisting of about a dozen men of mixed races, spread out in the grass fellowshipping. I am currently enrolled in the art class, where I'm learning to draw and paint. These are invaluable skills and they are also fun and therapeutic. And since the Lord, Jesus Christ, is a very important part of my life, I attend chapel services regularly. Here, the services are not constantly interrupted by lockdowns, many visitors also come to volunteer. They preach and teach with vigor and give inspirational sermons that I can hold on to.

Recently, I felt a little harmless envy when I learned that the sponsor of the Veterans group is Tony Dow who played (Wally Cleaver) in "Leave it to Beaver." I grew up with that show! I thought it was fantastic that someone like that was supporting the programs here.

Another highlight for me is the fact that we can go outside at night. Actually, all medium-security facilities offer night programming, but I have just never had the privilege until now. It used to be a dream. For years I have wished that I could go out and smell the night air, feel the night breeze blow against my face. I used to look out from my small cell window at the moon and the starts and just wish and dream. Now, here at Lancaster, I can finally experience the sky. I get to see the colorful sunsets, wild cloud patterns, and all that others so readily take for granted. I go out every chance I get!

The guards are also more respectful here. I haven't seen any of the mental or physical abuse that I've seen at other institutions. I am so thankful to be here. The environment is more open here in every respect. The inmates don't draw racial lines between themselves, the administration is more open-minded, and this is the most peaceful facility I've ever been on. It wasn't easy to remain disciplinary-free at the other places. Provocations come from the guards and other inmates on a regular basis at other institutions. But here, if you're doing what you're supposed to do, no one bothers you. Here, I can finally see the rewards of being disciplinary-free.

I believe the Lord has watched over me all of these years. I advise others who come here to take advantage of these programs, and improve their lives.

The Lord works in mysterious ways!

---

*Contemporary CDCR and the guards are a lot less tolerant of correctional officer collaborating with prisoners these days.

Larry May is a world traveler, but his body and spirit yearns for the southwestern desert where he first found beauty and solitude. May is a son, a brother, a father and a friend of many. He's blessed to have the love and support of his family and friends.

OPRAH WINFREY

"The real work is to discover who you are, and to use who you are in service of the world."

A Driving, Motivating Force

BY ALLEN BURNETT

I weighed 155 pounds. I stood 5'5," and was obviously small for my eighteen years of age in a predatory environment. There I sat on the floor, my chin resting on my knees and my back against the graffiti-sprawled, concrete wall. A wall that separated a rusty toilet from the rest of the men. The stale, recycled air was polluted with cigarette smoke and the monotoned voices of dozens of men overcrowded in a cell too small for its population—each struggling to hide their nervousness by laughing and exaggerating stories to kill time —while we waited for our names to be called for our day in court. Some spoke Spanish, some Vietnamese, but the funny thing is that everyone cursed in English.

I sat there, irritated, quietly waiting, watching. The holding cell was cold, the loud senseless talk maddening and the overcrowding musty. I felt like a sardine crammed into a can. To give you an idea, the holding cell was made for twenty people; in actuality, we doubled that . Along with the noise was the gross odor, a mix of stress, funk and ass—with a hint of disinfectant—the scent of jail.

I spent three hours in that once white room, reading and rereading old, peeling graffiti, counting cracks in the floor, and inspecting the variety of faces before my state-appointed lawyer, Mr. Goran appeared at the holding cell bars. His slender six-foot-four frame was topped by a grayish curly coif, and his ashy-white skin was draped sharply in a light-blue suit and expensive shinny shoes. I watched him search the holding cell for me as I navigated the crowd of bodies to make my way to the opposite side of the cell bars in front of him.

As if on cue, the room went quiet; there was no privacy to be found. This was our second meeting during the month that I had been jailed. I examined his face for any hint of good news, but there was none. Mr. Goran was stoic. He started to whisper as I leaned in closer; he didn't say hello, or ask how I was holding up. He was direct, matter-of-fact: "The district attorney has decided to seek the death penalty." There was no break in his voice, no feeling. "I will come by the jail later tonight to discuss our options." I remember immediately repeating his words in my mind, "*Our* options." I tried to process his statement, and he looked down at his watch and was gone—just as quickly as he had come. I watched him walk away; I watched as long as I could until he disappeared. I was afraid to turn around and have my emotions betray my mask. My heart pounded loud in my chest. I knew I was in trouble. My mind told me I was in trouble, and I was trying to keep my body from telling the rest of the world I was in trouble. I held the bars tight to keep me on my feet.

Somehow I found my place back on the floor. I placed my back against the wall and pulled my knees as close as I could to my chest. This time, I buried my head into my folded arms and did what any eighteen-year-old would do facing the death chamber.

For two years I waited for trial. During this period. Mr. Goran made many more of those trips to crowded holding cells. I thought of suicide more times than I could remember, but I couldn't even get that right.

The horrors of the county jail were a precursor to prison, a training ground, if you will. Prior to jail I had never been exposed to blatant racism. Jail introduced me to being called directly: "Nigger!" Not once or twice, but I had the word hurled at me so much that I used to joke that it was my middle name.

Jails and prisons are the breeding grounds for ignorance and racism. These are backward places where everything is segregated by race: the dorms, recreation, showers and the pay phones. The system encourages it, and the inmates enforce it. And every now and then there are those rare 'oops' moments where a deputy would open the wrong door during another race's time and all hell would break loose. Since day one of prison for me, it's always been open season against blacks. You learn quick not to get caught alone.

By the time I was nineteen-years-old, I'd been caught in the middle of two race riots, once coming back from church. I managed to get away with just a broken finger that round. I had been humiliated by a much bigger, older inmate who talked to me so bad you would have thought I came out of his testicles. I had also been choked, lifted off my feet by my neck by a deputy who, to this very day I believe was on 'roids. I learned a valuable survival lesson through that experience. If a deputy asks "Where are you going?" never respond with, "Where do you think I'm going?" It just isn't a good idea.

Before the age of twenty, I had some of everything you can think of thrown at me: scolding hot liquid detergent, hot chocolate, a bag of piss. There were other things, but I'll keep that between God and myself.

By the time I finally made it to trial, I was a walking, sleep-deprived, emotional wrecking ball. Not only was I challenged to focus on the trial, but I had not even begun to focus on why I was on trial in the first place. Trial lasted for a month, a blur of expert testimony, lay witnesses, stretched theories and an atmosphere of "every man for himself," all wrapped in an ill-prepared defense. Deliberation lasted two long, excruciating days, which resulted in a guilty verdict on every single count. I was sentenced to life without the possibility of parole.

The December night was cold as I arrived at the iron gates of New Folsom. The prison was hidden under the nighttime menacing shadows of the winter clouds. The place resembled a medieval castle. To this day people often grimace when I mention that I started my time there. I would describe the experience there as a "nightmare," but then cap it as my "alma mater." Sometimes I'd rationalize, "Everyone should start their time there." The truth is that Folsom was a scary place. But I survived the nightmare, and not only did I survive, but the experience taught me how to survive in prison. Folsom was the most violent, most predatory place you could dump a twenty-year-old first termer.*

Everything and everyone in Folsom seemed big to me. The weight pile was so huge that it looked like a full-scale construction site, with all the iron bars and plates laying around. The men there, inmates and guards alike, looked like they were made for the place—giants. In my young mind, everyone was on steroids. I couldn't wait to buy some in the canteen I figured, so I could be a giant, too.

I was one of three arrivals that night: Drew, Kiki and myself. Not one of us was over twenty-five-years-old, but each one of us had life without the possibility of parole. Drew was chubby, short, dark complexioned with shoulder-length dreads and pearly white teeth. He looked every bit of fifteen-years-old. By April he would be beaten and raped repeatedly by his cell-mate, a giant who called himself "Leah." When he finally found the courage to report the abuse to a nurse, his bravery was rewarded with a slicing from his mouth to his ear—for snitching.

Kiki was bi-racial (Black and Hawaiian) and a little slow. When the older guys saw him coming they used to say he had "sucker" written across his forehead. He was manipulated into being in charge of the safe keeping of dozens of illegal, pris-oner-made weapons. Later, as a major search was underway, he threw the knives away to avoid being caught with them. For this, he was stabbed repeatedly, for using what otherwise would have been a common sense decision.

While sad, I learned to take tragedy in stride. I confronted my own suicidal temptation. I lived with the death penalty hanging over my head for nearly two years. I withstood a grueling trial. I was sentenced to life without any hope of ever getting out. I'd experienced racism face to face. I'd seen the worst kind of violence, repeatedly, all before the legal age to buy beer.

There were no therapeutic groups in jail, or Folsom. There was nothing to help me transition from friends and family to a solitary life of confinement. There was nothing to set me on the right path, or even any incentive for me to program in a positive way. And at that point, I didn't care. I struggled emotionally, mentally and was a real stress and anxiety case. To add to it all, during my prison orientation committee, I was handed a letter from the district attorney that was placed in my prison file that stated, "Burnett was the driving, motivating force behind his crime and it is fitting for him to die in prison." That letter was the final peg that drove me to hopelessness.

Looking back, and now understanding the "fight or flight" response, being caged and confined, I didn't even have those options. There was nowhere to run, and no one to fight. Yet I was lashing out at everything and everyone, without understanding why.

My first years in prison were the hardest. I witnessed countless acts of violence, and drug abuse. It was common to see a slashing or sticking over an unpaid debt or prison politics. Alcoholism was the norm, to help guys cope, with suicide being the last option when the stress and loneliness were finally too much to bear.

I remember one Sunday a man hung himself. He was having problems with his marriage. The story goes that he received a letter from his wife. It was a Dear John letter explaining that she was leaving him for another man, and they were running off to Atlanta together. She believed he was a "good man" and deserved to know the truth about her affair.

We sat at the domino table and watched them rush his lifeless body on a gurney to medical. A nurse ran alongside the gurney, pounding away at his chest. The strange part about it was that not one of us were at all surprised, nor did we feel anything besides numbness toward the incident. That's when I realized what hardened meant. I also realized that to be otherwise was dangerous for us; the very emotion and sensitivity he yielded to, killed him. In a cold, heartless place like prison, investing in empathy, to just care, could prove fatal.

With a heavy sigh of relief, I left Folsom in 1997. As if jail wasn't enough, I survived two prison wars, a major race riot, all by the grace of God. The thing about wars and riots are that everyone becomes a target in these chaotic free-for-alls. The guy on crutches, the Hispanic with surrendered hands, the black guy all-ready injured and sitting in the dirt, anything in blue can be shot or otherwise subdued because the violence is fast. With the violence so fast, widespread, dusty and, or smoky, everyone is driven by instinct, survival instinct.

And despite the fact that I walked away from those incidents physically unscathed, these type of situations almost always result in mental and emotional trauma. I became more and more detached as the years passed. I never learned how to take responsibility for my crime, I just blamed everyone else.

I had become a grown child with new skills, and the muscle to never be any bully's focus – ever. But mentally, I was the same kid I was when I was arrested, just more tormented. I protected myself to whatever degree was necessary, including manufacturing weapons. It wasn't until I landed myself in the notorious Pelican Bay State Prison that I concluded that I needed to change my life around. It was four years later when I found myself on bedrock, fighting a weapon's case. Bed rock is a cell made completely of concrete with two cement bunks side by side. Imagine waking up in the hole, on bedrock, with another man laying arms distance from you. Not cool.

Despite how it looked, my cellmate was an older guy I'd met years before at Folsom. Owl was in his forties, tall, balding and built like a wide receiver – a giant. He didn't talk much initially, but when he did his speech was deliberate and focused. He personified respect when he spoke. Over the next four months I absorbed what he had to share. I learned that he'd been in since he was eighteen, too. He was also sentenced to life without parole. He started his time in the historic San Quentin in the bloody '8os. He told me many stories, like how he dealt with his father's death while serving hard time in Corcoran's security housing unit (SHU). He was so affected by the news that he lost it, and beat his cellmate half to death. Over the years he ended up losing all of his outside support, friends and family. To deal with his grief, he accepted his sentence and his fate to die in prison as if etched in stone. His stories became cautionary tales that made me reflect on my life, the bitterness that was overwhelming me, the violent path I'd chosen, the hopelessness I fed daily. I was the person the district attorney had said I was. I knew that wasn't the definition I wanted for myself.

I was twenty-seven-years-old when I left Pelican Bay. I ended my racist associations; I avoided conversations that promoted prison politics, and the violence that goes along with it. I enrolled in vocational classes, and found different ways to educate myself. I began to occupy my time with constructive activities, and gained a sense of accomplishment. It felt good. I managed to remain disciplinary free long enough to earn a custody reduction with zero negative points.

My counselor told me about a program in Los Angeles County that might fit me called the Progressive Programming Facility. Mr. Major was a Vietnam vet. He always had a story to share. He would sit in his office, his long legs stretched across the floor with is pale hand doodling as he talked, looking over his brown, wire-framed glasses. He spoke of his friendships in Vietnam, real friends, and what genuine loyalty is. He talked to me as if I were another human, not just an inmate with no value. Sometimes I would stop by his office just to experience an unbiased "real conversation." I liked that.

For the next two years he tried to get me to Los Angeles County, but it was always "closed to intake." I just kept on programming, doing my time as constructive as possible. Then, in 2010, I was finally accepted. My mistake was sharing the news with my co-workers, who responded with nothing but negativity. They called the Progressive Programming Facility a protective custody facility. I bit into the peer pressure, doing everything I could to get out of the transfer. I refused to go to a facility with a bad reputation, even on a positive path. My life sentence forced me to do everything in my power to hold on to a good, respectable name. It was all I had left. It only takes one time for someone to say you're "no good" and the probability for you to get stabbed shoots to 10. I was so obsessed about what others thought that I almost squandered a life-changing opportunity.

When Mr. Mayor found out about my attitude change, he called me in for one of those "talks." When I entered his office, he gave me a look of disappointment, removed his glasses – by pinching the nose-bridge. He leaned back in his chair in a long, exaggerated motion. It was hard for me to meet his gaze; I focused on his thinning hair.

I was embarrassed. I saw the inconsistency. Out of my own mouth, I'd claimed to want to turn, my life around, but my recent activities showed otherwise. I'd been cuffed up twice since my transfer approval, and each time I was sent back to my cell with a warning. They were giving me the benefit of the doubt. I'd been programming for so long, so well, in contrast to my past. It seemed everyone knew what was up, but me. I tried explaining my concerns. He listened patiently, even nodding empathetically. When I was done, he silently handed me my transfer papers and began reading off all of the programs the PPF had to offer.

I have practically grown up in prison. I have spent the latter half of my adult life raised between six maximum-security institutions: California State Prison New Folsom, Kern Valley, Tehachapi, Pelican Bay and Lancaster (Los Angeles County). The PPF was like nothing I could have imagined for prison; it was such a contrast to my previous prison experiences. Violence is rare, racism is completely absent, no more of those vicious melees in the middle of the yard where the only real winners are the pepper spray and gas canisters. Here, the yard tables and exercise bars are "owned" by no one, but shared by all, eliminating any tension whatsoever.

Here, men don't stab each other over some ill-perceived disrespect. No young Kikis are manipulated into stock piling weapons or carrying out some form of violent discipline at the call of an "older homie." At the PPF, youngsters are not raped by their cellmates, and no hopeless kids are considering suicide as an option. Here, they learn how to cope with their stress or feelings of abandonment.

It didn't' take me long to adjust to the PPF, the change came normal, as this is probably as close to mainstream thinking as we're going to get in any prison. The PPF encourages self-help and higher education.

I immediately enrolled on the college program. (We must pay for books and tuition.) Earning an associate's degree was an achievement I could only dream of, but never imaged any real opportunity to earn it in prison.

I also began participating in some of the self-help classes here, searching for personal growth. I learned about the peer-to-peer education group called the Men For Honor. The first course I took was the Victim Sensitivity class. This was the class where I learned about childhood traumas and the causative factors of my criminal behavior. This class, along with New Choices, Different Directions, a gang diversion class, and the Lifer class, helped me to understand the impact of my criminal acts. These classes taught me how to take responsibility for the harm I caused and how I could attempt to make amends. During my involvement with this pro-social group, I was able to make meaningful friendships within the group's executive body, and was soon accepted as a regular member of the Men For Honor. Later, I was given responsibilities as the group's coordinator, and now head the group as chairman. It is a real privilege, and the first positive group I've ever been involved with in prison.

The Men For Honor has essentially become a brotherhood to me; one based on true respect and solidarity. In the Men For Honor, we help build each other, instead of trying to cut each other down and destroy one another. Our aim is to guide one another toward healing, to make each other well-rounded as individuals.

We also strive to give back and support the local community. Recently I managed a fund-raiser for the Lancaster-based Children's Hospital. Now we are working on a fund-raiser for at risk kids. These achievements have given me a sense of self-worth, and have shown me that life is still worth living, even if restrained by an 8-by-10 foot cell. I don't think about suicide anymore. I don't think about hurting others anymore. I don't rely on self-destructive ways to cope, but have learned positive coping mechanisms to not only benefit me, but those around me.

One of those new coping mechanisms is instructing the Workforce Development class. With the benefit of a partnership with the Lancaster-based New Beginning Outreach, I use their curricula to help my peers learn to prepare for the job hunting process. Many people would be surprised to learn how needed such instruction is in prison. The experience has not only taught me how to dress and conduct myself during interviews, but also given me invaluable teaching and leadership skills. Under the Men For Honor, I have been able to help my peers on a mass scale, preparing them, and myself, to be contributors to our communities and our families. Twenty-two years ago I would never have imaged being in a place like the Progressive Programming Facility. Or being involved with a group of positive, like-minded men who practice giving to one another, not taking. Now I know my potential, I have found I have some direction and purpose, and it is a far cry from the image the district attorney described me to be when I was twenty-years-old.

---

* Assembly Bill 1276 was signed into law on September 27, 2014, by Governor Jerry Brown. This sensible measure was initiated by Elizabeth Calvin of Human Rights Watch. It mandates that youth and young adults (those under the age of 22) be housed in institutions with lower security levels and increased access to educational and self-help programs. Institutions where they are less apt to be manipulated, or as published by Human Rights Watch: "[To] prevent thousands of the state's youngest prisoners from being initiated into their incarceration with the experience of rape, assault and gang life."

Allen Burnett is a student at Cal State Los Angeles's offsite campus, majoring in Communication studies with an emphasis in Organizational Communications. He is a member of the WordsUncaged steering committee.

Burnett's *"Irreparable Good Man"* is featured in the 2017 Journal, *Human*. Burnett is currently sentenced to life without parole.

JOHN DEWEY

American Educator

"To lose faith in each other would be to lose faith in ourselves (and that is the unforgivable sin.)"

Living Life Without the Possibility of Parole

BY WAYNE MONTANIO

I am living on a medium-security facility, which could not have happened if the rules were not changed for people like me. You see, I was sentenced to life without the possibility of parole. For the past thirty years a person with such a sentence could only be housed on a maximum-security facility. It didn't matter whether I followed all the rules, never got into trouble or was a model prisoner, my sentence alone would condemn me to the harshest, most volatile of institutions.

It is the maximum-security institutions that are usually rife with petty, internal politics among the prisoners. In California, they are thick with racism and lockdowns because of the inevitable violence, lockdowns that can last for many, many months—even years at a time. It is these conditions that make a prisoner feel more like an animal than a human being. I will never look at a caged animal the same. The hopelessness, the despair, it is unbearable.

Then, one day, just like that! everything changed. In mid-2013 a study was conducted by the University of Sacramento that recommended that prisoners not be eternally condemned to maximum security solely for their initial crime—decades after they were arrested. The study concluded that prisoners often mature, change their thinking, change their behavior. There is a long pattern and history of lifers eventually becoming the most peaceful and productive of all prisoners. The study recommended that prisoners be able to earn their way to lower level institutions if their behavior is consistent with positive programming. I happened to be one of those who was eligible for a lower level institution, with less violence, more programming opportunities and, thank God, less lockdowns.

I learned about the Progressive Programming Facility not long after that, I learned of the study. I heard that all I had to do was sign-up, to volunteer. For a person who has never been to prison before; never been in a gang; never been a racist, I didn't know what to expect. Truth is, despite all of the good things I had heard about the PPF, I was still scared.

I really wanted to go to a medical facility. I have health problems that stem from military service in the 70's. I served in the Marine Corps from 1973 to 1977. I was released from service with an honorable discharge due to a badly damaged left knee. My knee suffered further deterioration later during my commercial diving career. As I grow older, the pain and discomfort intensifies, so I would rather avoid the wild riots and other violent activities as best I can.

I prayed about it and gave the situation to God. Soon after, I went to committee and faced the administration. I talked with them, they reviewed my history and to my extreme gratitude, I was approved for the PPF that same day. I signed the contract agreeing to all of the rules and I immediately began seeking out the programs.

On the yard, I saw many people that I had met at other institutions. They all welcomed me, and I was surprised to see so much respect and harmony among the prisoners. Race was completely irrelevant. That was something I had never seen before in prison. In every other prison I've been to, everything hinges on race. Here, blacks, whites, Asians and Hispanics were playing sports together, sharing religious activities and being completely open in group settings.

Various people told me about all of the self-help programs and classes available. I went from scared to excited. One of the classes I really benefited from was the Veterans' Group. The focus of this group is for veterans to help one another—inside and outside. Many of us still have issues from our service, and through this group we can confide in one another, we can express our issues and hear how others successfully overcome their issues, or at least cope with them. Veterans from the outside also volunteer to help and guide us with our unique needs.

The Men For Honor Lifers' class has also been a big help to me. It has given me direction as a lifer, as a prisoner with no hope. The class gave me direction as a lifer, as a prisoner with no hope. The class gave me an avenue to openly talk to others in my situation. It gave me my dignity and worth back, and gave me something to work toward. Men for Honor also offers Workforce Development, which is a life skills class that helps guys learn to fill out job applications, compose resumés and other skills needed to succeed after release. Just the positive setting was a benefit.

Paving the Way is a relationship class offered by a lady who volunteers to come in and instruct us. She challenges us to rebuild torn relationships, and helps us do this by giving us advice and approaches to reconciliation. We learn new ways of dealing with family issues that are more constructive than approaches some of us have used in the past.

The PPF has so many programs it is unbelievable. I still have Narcotics and Alcoholics Anonymous, Conflict Resolution, and so much more to attend.

I have met a lot of older men on this facility, men who are in their 60's and above. Many have been locked up for thirty-years-plus. These guys are mature, level-headed and I am happy to be here, learning and growing with them. God has made a way when it seemed there was no way!

This facility is such a positive force for change and rehabilitation. The PPF is a facility that supports and encourages men who have decided to truly change themselves. There is no other facility like this.

Wayne Montanio is a former actor/stuntman, but to talk with him gives no hint of the typical "Hollywood," personality.

Wayne is a humble spirit, generous and always striving for self-improvement. This ole service member, a proud Marine to be exact, likes to paint, practices sign language, mentors the youth and dabbles in creative writing.

Wayne is always sociable, patient and willing to lead or follow, whichever is appropriate for the occasion.

SPIKE LEE

"Power is knowing your past"

My Path Toward Redemption

DONALD MOSS

It all started in a Men For Honor class, the Victim Sensitivity class. On this particular day, we were talking about trauma, how trauma affected us at a young age. We discussed how trauma can change our thought patterns and behavior.

To me, this class was very thought-provoking. I was so intrigued by the issue that I needed to learn more. I went on a quest to find how my young life experience impacted my later days. First, I contacted the facility psychologist, who was very helpful in referring me to a book: *The P.T.S.D. Work Book*. The book enlightened me on the effects of trauma, and the different types of trauma. The book also suggests how to reverse the effects of trauma.

The first step in dealing with trauma is to recognize its impacts. A traumatic event has many possible impacts. It can impact your feelings, thoughts, relationships, behavior, attitudes, dreams and hopes (p. 3).

Your are either the direct victim (if it happened to you) or the secondary victim (if it happened in your world or you were a bystander or observer of a traumatic event.... However, you have seen enough to know that your exposure to awful events has impacted you significantly (p. 4).

I believe my trauma started at a very young age. My home life was dysfunctional and noisy. My father was a violent alcoholic. He would come home, and start arguing, and fighting with my mother. My older brothers and sisters would try to shield me from his madness, but I saw it many times. Before I was eight-years-old, I saw two murders in my neighborhood, and too many gun fights, and assaults to name. Violence was all around me. Even the police were unjust and abusive.

There was this one time; it was my first encounter with the police. I was around three-years of age in 1964. We only had one T.V. in our house. My brothers, sisters and I would sit around in the living room and watch *Soul Train*. On this particular day, there was a knock at the front door. My mother answered it. The police were there saying that there was a disturbance call from our house, but that wasn't true. We knew this because we were the only ones there. My father was at work that day. So my mother let the police know that there was no disturbance, and even let them in so they could see for themselves.

The police walked in, and walked straight over to where my brother, Eric, was sitting. They kicked his legs off the table. Eric stood up, and asked what their problem was. My mother got in between them, and the officer pushed my mother out of the way. My brothers and sisters jumped on the police, and it was on. I ran to the back yard and got our dog. But before I could get back to the living room my mother stopped me and Fred, our dog. No one was seriously hurt, but the police were clearly abusive. That incident had a very negative affect on me. I haven't trusted them, or any authority since. It was my very first encounter with the police, but definitely not my last.

Both of my parents worked. So it was up to my brothers and sisters to take care of me. I was the youngest of five siblings. One day I was coming home from school and I got jumped on by five guys. After getting beat down, I made it home. When my brothers learned what happened, they took me back to those guys and made me fight them again, one at a time. I was about ten-years-old then. Eventually, the constant exposure to gang activity pulled me in.

...[T]raumatic events have the ability to change anyone who experiences them. You have been changed in some, or many ways by your experiences of prolonged, repeated trauma, and those changes may be soul deep (p.197).

Traumatic experiences can rob you of your sense of self (p.16).

When exposed to violence at such an early age, it was only natural for me to be affected. By the age of twelve, I was completely involved in gang activity.

My brother, Tom, who is two years older than me, influenced me to take that path. I got involved in gangs because I was always around my brother, and he was in a gang. It was his job to look out for me, and I was the tag along. When he hung out with the fellas, I was right there. When he and the fellas would do mischief, I was right there.

The first thing he would say is, "You better not tell nobody." When I got jumped on, he was the one who taught me to get them back. There were times when we would get into it and we wouldn't stop until somebody got hurt. We wouldn't let anyone else get between us when we were fighting. If they did, we would go after them.

We would also fight our friends in the neighborhood the same way, and if they fought back, win, lose or draw, we'd let them in. This is how our gang started and grew. It was around 1972. Over time, our gang grew from five or six to thirty. We learned to show no fear, not to say there wasn't any fear. We just learned not to show it. We showed no fear, and no empathy because these emotions showed weakness. Weakness was not what we wanted to portray. We had to be tough, not only with outsiders, but within our group.

I ended up in juvenile hall where gang banging was rampant, and completely unchecked. In fact, the counselors would often turn their backs to our activities. In juvenile hall I learned that the more violent I was, the more accolades I got. It was the same in placement camp, and Youth Authority; there were no consequences for violence. I had no fear of jail, or prison, or the hole, because every time I was released, there was more respect; I was more accepted, and my reputation was greater. This type of attention made me feel powerful, more confident, and as crazy as all of this may sound, I felt safe around all of the violence and chaos. When I ended up in prison, there was nothing standing in my way. My anger and rage were in the perfect environment to be nourished.

Your *schemas* are your beliefs and expectations about yourself, others and your world. *Schemas* guide and organize how you process information and how you understand your life experience. Your *schemas* become your basic rules of life, if they are based on distorted information, they can lead to distorted ways to view yourself, others, and the world. Your strongest *schemas* are those that have been the most powerfully reinforced (p. 157).

I came to prison for a gang-related murder. I felt I had sacrificed my freedom in the name of the gang. I felt betrayed when other members flipped on me, and testified against me. Their betrayal increased my rage, and I doubled down on my activities and beliefs. Then it occurred to me one day that I have to change the way I think, feel and respond. After reading the P.T.S.D. book, I realized that I needed to change my negative beliefs to positive beliefs. I realized that I am worthy of love from the right woman. I am worthy of friendship with the right friends. I am worthy of happiness and success.

My quest for answers to what was driving me in that destructive direction was intrusive, but it gave me insight and was thought-provoking. I knew I had to unravel my destructive way of viewing myself and the world. This workbook offered me a positive outlook, a new way to see things, and help me understand my problems.

The person who works through a history of trauma and comes out the other side as a (somewhat) whole person, has certain character traits and abilities that can be learned or developed by using many of the exercises in this workbook, such as: to tolerate or lessen the intensity of painful feelings. Recognize self-blame, shame, and then counter it. Stay connected with persons who are both present and absent. Be alone without being lonely. Self-sooth when upset. Anticipate consequences of actions and events. Set and maintain appropriate physical and emotional interpersonal boundaries. Provide mutual self-support with supportive others. Have will power. Take initiative. Have empathy for others. Have a sense of humor (p.197).

Healing occurs when we are able to control our own behavioral responses (choosing when and how to express anger) (p. 198).

When I was very young, all of the trials and tribulations in my life were terrifying, and therefore traumatic. I realize now that I was scared during many of these incidents. As I got older, lashing out in anger became normal. Violence was my first response to solving problems. I refused to be the hunted, so I became the hunter. There was nothing stopping me. As a result, my entire adult life has been lived in prison.

The goal of working in this workbook has been to help you build psychological wellness. If you are psychologically well, you are able to maintain a healthy lifestyle that has balance in its physical (fitness, nutrition), social (relationships, support systems), emotional (self-worth, hardiness), vocational and educational (productivity) and spiritual (purpose, meaning, ethics, values), aspects (p. 217).

Maintain some sense of balance (p. 218).

This workbook revealed many emotional symptoms, which helped to guide me in bettering myself. I did not know change was needed. This workbook helped me to realize that I need balance in my life, and that I need not be emotionally numb.

The interest that the Victim Sensitivity class arose in me helped me to understand trauma better, and find a title for my problems. The class, and the book, helped me discover that my biggest problem is self. My past is written in stone, but my future is yet to be written. Now there will be some happiness, some joyfulness, some peacefulness and success. Change is coming.

In conclusion, the chains not only need to come off of my ankles and wrists, but also off my mind, so that I can become whole.

Master of others is a strength. Mastery of yourself is
true power.

--Lao Tzo

This is what I'm striving toward; the ultimate power of
oneself.

Sources:
The PTSD Work Book, by Mary Beth Williams, Ph.D, Soili Poi
Jula, PH.D. (New Harbinger Publications, Inc., Oakland, CA
2000)

BILL GATES

"Education is society's great leveler, and any improvement in education goes long way toward equalizing opportunity."

It Doesn't Have to End Where it Began

BY CLIFTON "LEE" GIBSON

The large 300-pound grill gate slowly opens in front of me, allowing access to the narrow, foreboding confines of the 20 foot long housing unit entrance. In prison, we call this the rotunda, a shadowy hallway to hopelessness, or even a death trap, if you're not alert.

By instinct, I have become conscientious of my surroundings, especially behind me. I make sure no one has followed me in. When I turn to look behind me, I see that I am alone. The involuntary release of my breath, and the loosening of my muscles indicate my inner relief. The grill gate's half-inch-thick bars reverse course, like a mouth closing, once I am in. As a final expression, the menacing gate closes and sounds off an unmistakable shutter as it locks, tight. It exhibits its own finality.

My concerns are not unfounded. I've seen prisoners get pounced on in these rotundas, others butchered, and both victim and victimizer mutilated by the high-powered rifles that respond to the insanity with live rounds. From peace to sudden violence, and from screams and hollering to gunshots, in the end, the bullet restores order.

Inside the confines of the wider housing unit, the gun ports not only cover the rotunda, but generously gives access to watching guns in every direction of the housing unit. Ominous is the word that comes to mind as I stare up into the potential maws of death that are called gun ports.

You never want the gun ports to be opened when you're standing below because when they do, a mini-14 follows, and its eye sees only to maim or kill—ricocheting bullets cannot discriminate between victim or victimizer.

The way out of the housing unit can be just as concerning. As I exit towards the yard, three heavily tattooed prisoners are 30 feet out, rushing towards me fast. My eyes search their hands looking for clenched shanks or closed fists. A complete scan of their faces offers some insight into their demeanor; it appears that they are trying to defy the security protocol, and enter without permission. I am relieved, but you never know.

I realize, as they flash by me, that I had taken the defensive measures of stepping aside and clenching my own fists. My heartbeat slows and my breathing relaxes as I continue under the intense, dry desert summer sun here at the California State Prison, in Lancaster. And without warning, shots ring out from the distance. Had my intuition been right all along? My stomach clenches, and my heart again races as I try to hone in on the location of the dust-up. But there is none. The guards are not running; they aren't shouting at us to "get down!" nor is there any swift, chaotic movement. It turns out that the guards are practicing at the gun range on the other side of the wall.

The yard is calm as runners pass by in front of me, and guys playing handball grunt to my left, and guys playing basketball shout scores to my right. Again, you never know.

The reality is, I am on the Progressive Programming Facility, and violent incidents like those described above are rare, if at all existent. The thing is, I didn't start my time here, and the traumatic experiences of the past keep me sharply focused. Focused on the potentially sudden eruption of violence that we call prison.

I head through the well-lit and narrow hallway, towards the class that sits in the very back of the building. I enter and find my regular seat. I feel the comfort of being surrounded by like-minded peers. Prisoners who desire to heal, who desire to reform themselves, who desire to make amends for their past transgressions. Our purpose is to walk toward a path of help-fulness, and to promote kindness.

In my experience, after twenty years of incarceration, prison isn't usually supportive of such goals. Not to mention being hunted by our pot-hole-filled road of bad choices, which at times can mentally derail any efforts at fulfilling such goals. Overwhelming guilt, and a new sensitivity to errors buried deep within the soul are addressed. My aim is the Advanced Catalyst Class, brought by a volunteer from the Creating a Healing Society, a non-profit in Lancaster. But first, I must get approved to pass the chain-linked gate that serves as a barrier to the services departments: Education, the Adminis-trative Offices, Clothing, the Library, and Canteen. The gate entrance is heavily guarded. I am confirmed on the class list and allowed to pass through, after being patted down, and checked for weapons or other contraband. I am cleared by a non-descript, "Go-ahead."

In Catalyst, we deal with, and confront, items like childhood trauma. How a traumatic childhood event might have overwhelmed our ability to cope, which in turn can lead to what behavior specialists call "trauma re-enactment." The purpose of this introspection isn't to make excuses for our crimes, but to search for the turning point towards criminality, and get to the bottom of our issues. Our instructor and guide will not allow us to shirk our responsibilities, encouraging, pushing us to dig deep. Dave, a tall, slender gray-headed man, urges us to excavate beyond our regret, and dig past the many emotions that underlie the ugliness of our past mistakes. Dave possesses an inviting, approachable spirit. He is kind, but firm, and while his thinness makes him seem small, he is actually big on expectations and knowledge.

In an environment of hatred and victimization, Dave sees past our coping masks, he sees the inner being, that wounded child desperate for healing. I've made great progress under his tutelage. Dave has helped me fill many of those deserted potholes with insight of my triggers and remorse for my wrongs. Dave is our sensei for Creating a Healing Society.

The healing comes from the difficult task of dealing with our traumatic experiences, and confronting the toxic feelings that emerge as a result. This work, this very hard work, as opposed to acting out those feelings in the usual anti-social and self-destructive ways, has its own internal and external rewards. Prisons are a concentrated caldron of warped thinking, and Catalyst helps us to rise to the challenge of the unfamiliar by practicing morality and integrity. Despite the challenge, Catalyst is well worth it. Transient pain for long-term healing.

My many incidents of shame, embarrassment, and other trauma as a child were the foundation of my warped views, and the debilitating confusion that was my companion for most of my young life. These were the constant trade winds that kept me veering off to the left in my life, that kept me from becoming the potentially productive member of society that I was meant to be. I realize now that I was supposed to be contributing to society through constructive work product, and paying taxes like other hard-working Americans. I was supposed to be creating a family, and raising well-mannered kids. While I am a very different person now, I realize that I am still the sum of my experiences. But my motivations and aims have changed direction.

Now I am driven to help others to find what I have found, to contribute, and help produce contributors. My drives and passions are now funneled through the concepts of morality, founded on societal standards, not street codes, and underground leanings.

I am the first to admit that I am a damaged being. But that's what healing is about. And it isn't just Catalyst that has helped to heal and cure. The Progressive Programming Facility has exposed me to all types of self-help courses. Thanks to an agreement between the State and Coastline Community College, I have taken courses such as Sociology and Biology. Courses that have taught me discipline, and shown me that I can operate on society's level.

During my childhood, I was never really my own man. Unfortunately, I had a lot of negative influences, and those negative influences etched themselves very deep into my interior. But here on the PPF I have been given the space to become my own man. I have watched myself develop and mature on a level needed to pursue my passion for helping others, and fixing myself. Classes such as parenting have given me the skills to advise and guide at-risk youth, and even my peers. Every class and group I've joined has added to my personal repertoire in one meaningful way or another. For instance, I speak clear and confident now. I don't have to pretend to know something to feel esteemed. If I don't know, I admit that and try to improve in that area. I have also learned that it is okay to vulnerable. When I get nervous, I know that is normal.

I would probably have never realized how my childhood shaped me without these courses, and without the facilitation of the PPF for these opportunities. I would probably have never realized how my shame, fear and need for acceptance laid at the foundation of my past bad choices. Classes such as Houses of Healing, another course that guides people to explore past trauma, and Victim Sensitivity, which helps us realize the depth of our harm, and how we traumatized others have helped me grow tremendously. The Anger Management and Conflict Resolution classes were also pivotal in showing me how to properly deal with the daily hassles of life.

Creative Thinking class furthered my growth in that area by showing me how to think outside of the box, and not rely on old modes of seeing things. I learned to view problems as challenges and conflicts that are inevitable, but not personal. Narcotics Anonymous has provided me with the tools necessary to defeat chemical dependency. I am in a class full of guys with similar experiences, who have shared proven ways of overcoming. I also learn from their mistakes, and at times have been able to assist them in their recovery. All of these new experiences have guided me in a new direction, with victorious outcomes and a positive frame of reference to draw from.

These classes here on the PPF help me recognize, identify, and deal with the taxing, emotional, and traumatic experiences that I have dragged behind me like heavy luggage for so long.

In fact, these experiences help others to recognize value and leadership in me. In mid-2013, I was asked to join the executive body of the Men For Honor ILTAG. I serve as secretary. The Men For Honor is headed by men who have made a stance against the stagnant, aimless, worthlessness of normal prison culture. Combined, the executive body, the peer-instructors, and members bring a vast amount of knowledge, experience, and drive to make a positive impact on the population here. Hundreds and hundreds of men have benefited from these classes, and groups, as well as staff. Any time a population of negative, self-destructive, and hopeless people can be guided away from reliance on violence, and led away from fatalistic perspectives, the staff are less likely to have to confront harmful, or even deadly situations. In fact, in the ten years that the Honor Program and Progressive Programming Facility have been in existence, we have never had an all-out racial riot. That is a fact even the lowest level facilities cannot lay claim to.

Speaking for the Men For Honor, our aim is to help others realize their potential to become productive members of society, while constantly making the necessary corrections in our own lives. We are growing by the day, and the more success we have the greater number of success stories we have to offer.

As the Catalyst class ends, and we are dismissed, we all say our good-byes and file out across the yard, back to the awaiting trap we call the rotunda.

Clifton "Lee" Gibson was released in May of 2019 after serving approximately twenty-five years of a sentence of life without the possibility of parole for the senseless and tragic murder he committed when he was seventeen-years-old.

Understanding that he could never undo the harm he caused, Lee has vowed to never hurt another human being.

He has changed his past negative behavior into now exemplary life-long work in dedication to helping others. Lee is currently Secretary/Programs Specialist of the Men For Honor Group, he instructs Helping Y.O.U.T.H. (Helping Youth Offenders Understand Their Harm), and recently facilitated a guidance seminar for his students conducted by Human Rights Watch. He also offers guidance for at-risk youth sent to hear him, and other members of C.R.O.P. (Convicts Reaching Out to People) from the courts, and concerned citizens.

His mission is to contribute to an environment that promotes positive change for himself and others. He also mentors at-risk youth through letters, in hopes of stopping the cycle of violence that so ravages California communities. Contact Lee if you would like to assist him or support his endeavors.

"Light came to me when I realized that I did not have to consider any racial group as a whole, God made them duck by duck and that was the only way I could see them."

--Zora Neale Hurston

Hope: A Confident Expectation

BY LORENZO FLORES

My name is Lorenzo Flores. I am thirty-eight-years-old, and I am of Mexican-Korean and Apache heritage. I look like, and am viewed as Mexican. I have been incarcerated in the California Department of Corrections for seventeen years, since 1996. I am serving three life sentences for two attempted murders and one conspiracy to commit murder.

Sounds awful, doesn't it? And it is, however, in spite of my perpetual sentences, and the gravity of the charges, I am grateful that no one in my case was physically hurt. I sincerely thank God for that.

Believe me, I am not trying to make excuses for my actions. I was a troubled child. I was abandoned by my mother at age two, and abused by my father during my pre-teen years. Once the State took custody of me – for my own good – I was passed around from home to home, with more foster parents than I can name in this short testimony. I had some horrible experiences that helped shape my life, but ultimately, I knew right from wrong, regardless.

By 1996, I had reached twenty-one years of age, but I was still immature and misguided in many respects. I got lured into the gang life around this time, seeking the love, stability, and family I never really had. The violence that surrounded me also convinced me that I really didn't have much of a choice, at least it seemed that way. And once I came to prison, well, that was it. Where was I gonna hide?

Inside, as an Hispanic, and from a southern California gang, I was expected to represent: protect, defend, and further the aims of the clique. That involved beatdowns and other violence, race separation, drug dealing, and whatever else was necessary to strengthen politics – prison politics. In many respects, prison is about victimizing or being victimized.

I learned through experience that this path only dug me deeper into the very void I was trying to fill by joining the gang in the first place. Looking back, I was really living out a fatalistic attitude. With so much time, I had no hope. I thought my life was over and I had nothing left to live for. What was the use? What worth did I have? Here I am doing more time than people who have raped or molested children, or actually killed people.

The loneliness itself was unbearable, no matter who is there for me on the outside. After I shook off my personal, pity party, I came to realize that all was not lost. I began to open up to God. My hope was slowly beginning to renew, along with my inner strength. One day I believe I actually saw His mercy supernaturally, as it played out in my life.

On November 5, 2010, I had a dream. In this dream, a light shined out of the top locker, and on to me. There was what looked like a big iPhone in my dream that was emitting this strange light. I interpreted that to mean that I was being called from the light above. I went back to sleep.

I woke up again, around 5:30, much earlier than usual. Still, I got up, did my morning ritual with coffee, et cetera. It was so early; darkness still had a hold on the morning. My cellmate was still sound asleep. I sat down, and just stared straight ahead, my mind as blank as a sheet of paper. And again, just like in the dream, a bright light shined on me from the top locker. So I shot up and looked out of the window to see if the night guard was shining the light. There was no one there. I shook it off, and chalked it up as my being sleepy, or trippin'. I returned to my bunk and continued to sip my coffee.

I had been clean from drugs for about a month, but the temptation, and availability were there. Fighting for sobriety is hard, and in prison you're on your own, so it is even harder. I am still lost in my thoughts when the light shines from above again, but this time the light was more intense, and covered a wider space. The folded, hanging clothes on the wall made it look like the light was coming from inside the clothes. I jumped up to frantically search through the clothes, but there was nothing there. I thought I was going crazy, but before I could go on, I was interrupted by the television. The timer had come on, which was normal, but there was a Christian show on. There was no volume, but the captions – in large letters that read: "PSALM 112." I got spooked and turned the TV off.

I was stunned, confused. I got back on my bunk and wondered what it all meant. I decided to read the Scripture that was being displayed, to see what it said. I grabbed my Bible, a Bible I had never opened before, and the first thing the verse said was: "Praise the Lord!" I was encouraged enough by that to read on: "Blessed is the man who fears the Lord, who delights greatly in His commandments ...." The more I read, the more it blew my mind. As I got to verse four, it read: "Unto the upright light arises in the darkness ...." I was in shock.

I told God that He had my attention. Then I prayed repeatedly. From that day forward, my battle with addiction was conquered. In addition, I had been diagnosed with hepatitis-C, a disease that is pretty much incurable. They can suppress it, but its success rate is around forty percent.

I had been scheduled for interferon treatment, which really takes a toll on the body. Shortly thereafter I was scheduled in late November 2010. I was called to get one last check to see if the treatment would require a six- or twelve-month plan. My results came back completely negative of the disease. The reading was absent of any viral lode, whatsoever. The doctor was so baffled that he sent me to a hepatitis specialist for further tests.

The specialist refused to test me further after reviewing my blood work and on my last visit the specialist sternly, but in a joking manner, told me to get out of his office. He said that I didn't need to be there. I was shocked and confused. "Excuse me," I said. He looked at me straight on, gave me a wide smile and said, "Sir, this office is for the people with hepatitis, and you don't have it." As I turned away, he continued, "I know you had it, based on your antibodies, but your last test shows an absence of the disease in your body." I immediately gave credit to God, and called it a "miracle." God cured me!

I shared all of that to say that I was already open for change, but the environment I was in didn't offer much room for self-improvement. Not long afterward, I came across an article called, "My Shawshank Redemption," by Dortell Williams.* The article described the Honor Program at the state prison in Lancaster, California. Dortell described a prison environment that was perfect for someone like me, someone looking for a positive place to encourage personal change. He described a place, a prison with little or no violence, no racial or gang politics, and more programs than I could count.

I began to pray that I could go to that place in Lancaster. My prayer had been answered within two and a half years. I arrived here at the Honor Program on July 3, 2013. It was just in the nick of time. I was transferred out in the midst of an on-going race riot.

After years of chaos, riots and so much violence, it takes a while to re-adjust. When I got here, I continued my habit of looking over my shoulders, and being on high alert for the slightest hint of trouble. It also took me a while to adjust to the absence of colorlines. It was okay to hug a brother from another race, or play sports with someone who has a different skin color. Many people I knew from other prisons, who had been here for a while, helped me to adjust by reminding me of how open the Honor Program is. After seventeen years of constantly watching my back, it isn't easy to just ... relax.

The Honor Program has since been renamed the Progressive Programming Facility. The PPF is still prison. There are many rules, and here we are held to an even higher standard. But we are still deprived of the every-day things that many people take for granted outside of these walls. We are still separated from our families. We are still deprived of most of the things we like and love. And we must share a very small cell with another man, a stranger. All in all, we are still confined, deprived and suffering. But the positive activities, the absence of violence, prison gang rules, and negative pressures are not here to distract us from self-help programs like at other prisons.

Now I find myself free enough to play cards with a black brother, a former Crip, in the dayroom. It's peaceful. As a

Christian, I now have the freedom to openly walk the yard with a Muslim friend. And one of my most memorable days was when I played basketball with teams made up of three different races – something not even imaginable at any other of the five facilities I'd been at before. In fact, that same week someone from a different race shared their food with me in the dining hall, an offense that could have gotten me stabbed at any other place.

Before I knew it, a friend who did time with me at another institution signed me up for a couple of Men For Honor classes: Lifer class, the Victim Sensitivity Awareness class, and Creative Writing. The Lifer class gave me focus on my responsibilities as a life-term prisoner. The Lifer class helped me address some of my faulty thinking. The Victim Sensitivity class taught me what empathy is, and how to empathize with others. It taught me how to feel remorse for my wrongs, and not just my direct victims, but for my offenses against society as a whole. Creative Writing, I love that class. That class re-awakened my youthful passion for poetry and story-telling.

There are so many other programs, apart from Men For Honor, too. I even signed up for yoga! Yoga, of all things. Yoga helped me to eat and live healthier. Yoga eased my back problems. The yoga class is taught by a peer named Mike Simmons, who has been instructing yoga, and many of the health-oriented classes, for years. Most all of the self-help classes are peer taught. Our classes cost the State nothing, and like most therapeutic groups, the sick relate to the sick, and help one another heal.

The Men For Honor group is an Inmate Leisure Time Activity Group, which means that prisoners are allowed to create and develop the program or activity, and a staff member is selected by the administration to monitor and give input. So the PPF and the peer-to-peer instruction works because it is all voluntary. Most inmates that come here want to come, like I did. And they come with passion and drive, lots of it.

There are also volunteers who are allowed to come on the compound to instruct. One of the first classes I took from the Friends Outside volunteer was Creative Conflict Resolution. It was a ball of fun! The instructor made it fun, while giving us many "tools" to be successful. For three days we were offered a variety of ways to resolve conflict. We exercised "venting" avenues. As a group, we were allowed to share personal coping methods, and other choices for overcoming conflict. Even long after the class, the bonds that were developed in that class, and many others, have lasted way beyond our short class experience.

I am currently on the Friends Outside Positive Parenting waiting list. Yes, I said "waiting list." All of these classes have waiting lists, and guys endure a lot just for a chance to attend these classes.

Now that I've fully adjusted to the program, and its uniqueness, I have fully integrated myself into it. Recently I was asked to translate the Narcotics/Alcoholics Anonymous sessions. When I first began attending AA/NA classes, I was very outspoken about my struggles with addiction. I enthusiastically shared how I was freed from my addictions. There are others in the group who knew me during my addiction, and recognized the change. It was at this time that I was offered the honor of serving as the vice-chairman of our chapter.

I also was asked by the Men For Honor executive body to instruct their Sharing of Language class, a class designed to help people of all cultures get a better grasp of the English language. All of this has given me self-worth and usefulness.

The chapel services are also great. I was able to enroll in the Channel Islands and Seminary College, based in Oxnard, California, as well. Channel Islands offers a correspondence program that allows participants with a GED, or high school diploma, to earn up to a doctorate. The school relies on donations, and the Protestant chaplain serves as proctor to verify our work and required hours. I really feel like I'm growing here, learning how to help myself and others. And it really helps to have other prisoners who have the same mindset and are supportive.

Though I am in prison with three consecutive life sentences, I feel blessed to be on a facility with so many positive individuals. Now, when I get up in my cage each morning, and I see the confining walls of my punishment, I can do so knowing that my life isn't being wasted by an idle, destructive existence, but a constructive, meaningful time that builds and contributes to my small world, and the larger world beyond.

---

*Dortell Williams' article, "My Shawshank Redemption," was originally published by the *Christian Science Monitor* at: http://www.csmonitor.com/2008/1110/p09s02-coop.html and can be found on p.163.

Lorenzo Flores is a big, smiling man with a huge funny bone. He is always laughing and joking, spreading humor like a contagion. He loves dogs, as is apparent with his work in PAWS For Life. Flores is a loyal friend who doesn't sweat the small stuff, "Let it go," he's likely to say. Even on his not-so-great days, he avoids confrontations and arguments.

Flores is a fun-loving soul. He gets animated about his football team, the Miami Dolphins, and all the kid comes out of him when electronic games are mentioned. Flores is a hardworking teammate, always willing to listen and share, an unsung humanitarian.

NELSON MANDELA

"People must learn to hate, and if they can learn to hate, they can be taught to love, for love comes more naturally to the human heart than it is opposite."

The Mask

BY DAMON R. MATHEWS

It is easier to sew two pieces of cloth together than to pull them apart. Besides, once that cloth is torn apart, the fabric will never be the same.

As children, we were all innocent. The paradox is that we were being raised in a chaotic world. At the beginning, we were filled with wonder, and trust came naturally. Entering into adolescence, we were faced with different challenges that went beyond trust. There were deceptive girls, violent bullies, and dangerous drugs out there. The way we deal with these pressures helps to shape our personalities. The anxiety that comes with being a teenager can be overwhelming. In addition, having a support system in place is one of the most important things during that time. The better the support system, for example, parents, teachers, clergy, the more likely our child-like innocence will remain.

Without that village of support, the teen begins to change for the worse. He will start to sew on a mask to help him navigate the minefields of adolescence. This is typical and I have seen it occur in my neighborhood, and others repeatedly. I was one of those adolescents that became an incarcerated statistic.

As the youngest, skinniest, and nerdiest sibling, I was more susceptible to the bullies and gang banging tough guys, who were all too willing to take advantage of my innocence. I was, without question, on the wrong end of many confrontations that resulted in my harm. I had had enough of playing the unpopular role as a soloist in my "hood," so I put on the mask of a gang banger. I began to act like, look like, and become just like the social miscreants I had so detested before.

I traded my innocence and blamelessness for the ability to fit in. My strategy was to wear the mask, while distancing myself from the bloody violence that came with the territory. Needless to say, that faulty plan was destined to fail from its conception; it eventually landed me at the front gates of prison.

There is a code of conduct gang bangers are expected to follow in California's maximum security prisons. Behind the encircling electrified fence is a locked-in atmosphere of dog-eat-dog violence and victimization. However, an outsider might be surprised to learn that when a gangbanger is stabbed, it is less likely to be done by someone of another race or gang. More often than not, the victim is going to be attacked by someone in his own gang or race. They call this being "disciplined." The reasons for discipline can range from stealing (because there really is honor among thieves), to snitching, to backing down from a fight. Other prison rules that can get a member disciplined are failing to pay personal gambling, or drug debts, or any form of homosexual activity, even flirting with another homeboy's woman.

Following these prison rules came easy to me, but somewhere along the way, I went from merely following the rules, to enforcing them. I went from being a newly incarcerated, scared twenty-year old, convicted of second-degree murder, to a thirty- two year old man, making and distributing shanks, and ordering other gang members to be disciplined. In other words, I went from being the skinniest, nerdiest kid, to calling shots. I found myself not only being highly respected among my peers, but also feared. The funny thing is that it was all a mask. I was playing a game of survival that somehow elevated me to levels never before imagined.

The pros to wearing the mask and wearing it well, was the bullies left me alone. The cons were that I found myself hurting other human beings. I also became a focal point for the prison guards. Looking back, I took way too many trips to the "hole." Not to mention being placed in the inevitable position of having to order an ally be attacked. Then there was the constant stress and fatigue; keeping up the façade was exhausting. Worst of all, I spent way more years in prison than necessary, before finally being found suitable for parole.

All I wanted was a life free from gangs, violence, and conflict. Yet I ended up getting even deeper into the culture than the average miscreant, all because of my wayward thinking, and bad choices. After fourteen years in prison, I was finally ready to take the mask off. I was more than ready, actually, I no longer wanted to live by the self-destructive rules and codes I disagreed with. One day while sitting in the hole, the thought occurred to me that I was knocking on death's door. Continuing on the path I was on would eventually lead me to kill somebody, or I would end up murdered. I could not imagine dying in a cold, hard, listless cell.

It was a frightening peak into my possible future, and it was not pretty. Tony Robbins, the successful motivational speaker, once said: "Everything you and I do, we do out of our need to avoid pain, or our desire for pleasure." My decision to get out of the gang life was motivated by my desire to avoid the pain of inevitable death. Mr. Robbins had hit the nail on the head, and I related to his way of thinking.

Yet a funny thing happened on my way to "Squares Ville." Although the mask was easy to put on, taking that bad boy off was an entirely different story. Telling the people most loyal to me – as a gang member and leader—that I was no longer interested in that lifestyle created its own problems. Then there was the matter of shedding the gang-banging mentality. The whole act had become my reality. Thinking, acting and behaving like a normal person, like a law-abiding citizen, after years of being an outlaw, proved to be more challenging than I could have ever imagined. I found myself repeatedly falling back into the familiar dark conduct in which I had grown accustomed.

It was like those two pieces of fabric. The mask I wore became a part of me. I could not just, unzip it and take it off. It took effort to remove it; a lot more effort than it took to put it on. I eventually had to tear it off. The work necessary to remove the mask required the appropriate tools, social and emotional tools, such as insight and critical thinking. No matter how genuine my motives were for change, I repeatedly failed because I lacked these tools. I was more than willing to obtain the training, and counseling necessary to adopt these social skills, but again the State Prison at Pelican Bay had no such programs available.

The void caused me to relapse more times than I could count.

I kept reverting to the tools of bullies, and gang-bangers. It was both hopeless and frustrating. A few years later, I found myself being called by God. The Bible and its life prescriptions helped me live more cleanly. Prisoners tend to respect a sincere conversation, and that relieved me of a lot of pressure. My new path allowed me to remain disciplinary free long enough to earn a transfer to the State Prison in Lancaster. The PPF is among the unique institutions in California, with its wide array of self-help programs. When I arrived here, there was a licensed psychologist who volunteered to teach anger management and a "lifers group." Participating in these programs put me on the right track, and offered me the tools needed to succeed. The mask was beginning to tear apart.

The PPF was where I was fortunate enough to be introduced to the Men for Honor ILTAG. This group of progressive thinking prisoners embodies what CDCR should be about. They offer Victim Sensitivity; resume writing workshops, parenting classes, and so much more. The programing that this group, and others offer this facility, and the state for that matter, is immeasurable. I was so impressed with Men for Honor, and what they do, that I decided to join them.

Thanks to my experience and participation in the many self-help groups offered through Men For Honor, and the PPF as a whole, I now have the conflict resolution and critical thinking skills needed to overcome the social and emotional challenges that plagued me most of my life. Ripping that terrible mask off was painful, but worth it. Moreover, as we all know, when something is torn it is never the same.

I have seen and experienced too much to ever be considered "innocent"; however, with each passing day more and more, I can feel the trusting pre-mask Damon being revived after being buried for so long. Having a reputation as a tough guy made me feel brave, but there is nothing more courageous than being your authentic self.

Damon strives to serve God, and his fellow man. He is more comfortable writing than he is speaking, but when he does speak, he wants his words to be meaningful. Today he leads by example and is always willing to listen.

MARK TWAIN

"Habit is habit, and not to be flung out the window by any man, but coaxed down stairs one step at a time."

Hope Resurrected

BY F. MILLSAP

Prison, in and of itself, is a horrible place. Yet, what I have found here is that any place can be what a person chooses it to be. I used to regard prison as a bitter and hopeless environment. I had heard many stories about prison since I was a youth, but those stories could never have prepared me for the reality of what prison really is.

I was just nineteen-years-old when I first set foot inside of the confining walls of a cell. If I had any residual hope at that time, it died as hopelessness solidified within my consciousness as that steel door closed, and locked behind me. It was as if, when that cell door closed, an overwhelming sense of finality was sealed with its lock. It was as if my life had ceased. My life had ceased in a way that would no longer allow growth or progression. I felt as though I had no reason to grow because this four-walled enclosure had become like my own personal sarcophagus, where my mind was mummified, and only the body existed. For my young mind, it was incomprehensible that the harsh fate of serving a lengthy sentence had become my personal reality.

Almost immediately I observed that violence was the preferred solution to conflicts. Despair was the prominent characteristic, while any leaning toward rehabilitation of self-betterment were conspicuously absent. My rationale for these pervasive, destructive attitudes was that the environment itself did not encourage change. So, overall, why should there be any hope for it?

As time elapsed, I gave in to hopelessness and its stranglehold. I found myself driven by a mindless conformity to the negativity, which surrounded me like a thick cloud. I intentionally, and defiantly, resisted any form of authority. I purposely engaged in violence toward others that resulted in many stints to administrative segregation, or what we call the hole. Instead of "corrections" being a place where I reformed myself into a better person, I had allowed the environment to transform me into a bitter person. I saw absolutely no light at the end of the tunnel.

My first cellmate did absolutely nothing with his time. He slept and watched television to pass the time away—to pass his life away. This was my first example of a sort of living, that wasn't' really living at all. His attitude was very negative, negative to the core. He kept the windows blocked and the cell dark, like a cave. Not once did I ever see him pick up a book, and he definitely couldn't read in the dark.

Our conversations consisted of war-stories from his early days in prison, and the future violence and negativity that he looked forward to. It was in this environment that my attitude towards the future was shaped and guided toward sheer hopelessness.

I faced nothing but darkness and deprivation in the cell, on the yard, and wherever I went. Negativity became a permanent fixture in my mind. Even the ways in which I did seek self-improvement were corrupted toward a negative end. I exercised for the sole purpose of using my body as a weapon, instead of for personal health. The books I chose only helped to radicalize my negative mentality.

I felt myself becoming a person that I did not recognize in the mirror, nor like. One day, I received a letter from my dear grandmother expressing her continued hope in me. She shared her faith that one day I would be released as a man worthy of the freedom I would receive. It was thought-provoking, and while my environment was still dark, her letter offered me hope. I began to read a lot about history, and I took a liking to philosophy. Both helped to change my perspective, and caused a lot of self-reflection. I began to question the type of person I wanted to be. In time a light began to glimmer from a distance, but it hadn't reached my heart and mind.

I came to the realization that I did not want to resign my life to one of hopelessness, anger, and resentment. I decided not to become like so many others I had previously looked up to. I had witnessed too many of my peers lose their minds to the poison of despair. I had seen too many fellow prisoners give up on any hope of self-improvement, they became stuck in a state of arrested development. I chose to rebuff the erroneous, underground system of illogic. I stopped in my tracks to make the decision to be a conscious determiner of my own fate.

While my mind was made up as to the direction I wanted to go, the avenues toward that path, or any tools to help facilitate that type of mindset were still absent. I walked on eggshells for years, searching for a way.

Eventually, I found that way at the State prison in Los Angeles County. That way is known as the Progressive Programming Facility, and is designed for prisoners who make the decision to take responsibility for their past, and their futures. For me, the PPF stood as an opportunity to pursue positive endeavors without the hindrance of negative influences. The PPF stood as a chance to regain my individuality, rather than being a mindless follower. Or constantly having to contend with negative peer pressure. The PPF served as an opportunity to shift my perspective from a socially irresponsible person, entrenched in the gang-subculture, to a person of integrity; a person who respects social norms and standards.

As a part of the PPF, I am able to participate in peer-taught, self-empowerment classes that are facilitated through various inmate-led groups. In these groups, such as Men For Honor, we place emphasis on improving ourselves and transforming our circumstances.

The first class I took was the MFH Creative Writing course. I wasn't' very enthusiastic about going, but I enjoyed writing so I went to see what the class had to offer. What I was exposed to was an enriching environment that was both encouraging and positive. Those facets drew me in for greater participation. It was that class that revealed to me that this place is not prison as usual, but that the PPF has a different tone.

The class that inspired me most was the MFH Victim Sensitivity class. From the very first session I became aware that I was viewing my situation all wrong. I learned that I had not only victimized others by my actions and attitude, but I had also victimized myself. I was made aware of what my true role as a responsible citizen was supposed to be. I was suddenly surrounded by others who not only shared this concept, but promoted it. Finally, I was surrounded by a mindset that had a positive, focused understanding, and that understanding garnered my heart. I was given a new sense of compassion and empathy that I had never experienced before. The class directed us to look into the reasons why we committed our crimes, and learn to have empathy for others.

I have also participated in the MFH New Choices, Different Directions class, which focuses on alternatives to the gang lifestyle, and more productive approaches to life. Outside entities, such as Friends Outside, also offer classes such as Creative Conflict Resolution, which helped me deal with conflict in constructive ways. Overall, we seek solutions to the problems that plagued us in our communities, and caused us to come to prison. I have gained valuable insight into my anger, and how I release it in healthy ways. I have new channels, positive channels for which to express anger now. I have gained valuable tools that are essential for my personal growth and eventual re-entry into society.

The PPF, and the inmate-led groups, are the ultimate contrast to all of the other prisons I have seen. This positive, encouraging facility affords individuals like me the opportunity to escape the petty prison thinking that often defies logic and societal standards. Negative conformity and peer-pressure are absent here, and each person is guided to be responsible for his own decisions.

At thirty-one years of age, I embrace the opportunity to be a participant in such a unique and successful program. It is without question a privilege to be among other prisoners as equally committed to positive change. I now understand the rewards of structure, order, and the individual gifts others have to impart. Their experiences have set me on a path to new and positive experiences of my own, and will definitely be useful upon my re-entry into society.

It is my sincere belief that the seeds that are planted in my heart and mind through these programs will bear fruit in society. The result of my journey so far has been the development of hope—hope in the future, hope in myself, hope in society. I know that I am proof certain that great change can occur when people are given the opportunity, the means and the methods for positive change. The PPF and its programs exemplify all of these things.

Fernando Millsap is a native of South Los Angeles. He enjoys writing poetry, reading philosophy and allowing his mind to wonder and ponder the immense possibilities of life. He is a lover of all types of music. If it has rhythm Millsap loves it. When he gets out of prison he hopes to start a family and counsel young people about the perils of the gang lifestyle.

A Second Chance

BY JOEL N. AGUILAR

"Tranquility is the first necessity for one to do well"

--Claude Monet

I see him in the exercise yard, both palms pushing his body off the ground. His head shaven directly a few feet below the barrel of a mini-14 slouch in a twenty-foot gun tower. I flank to the right, heading toward Eddie.

I round through the track when I spot him, this time, on the pull-up bar, his head cresting the cross bar. I snake around the herd of inmates, thrusting myself faster and faster, rousing some prisoners in alarm.

"Eddie, have you heard the good news?"

His face stiffens with that apathetic stare I've come to recognize too well from prisoners who have lost all hope in the system. For him, life without the possibility of parole is like a death sentence – regardless of what the provision of Senate Bill 9 says about getting a second chance for those who committed their crime as juveniles and were sentenced to life without the possibility of parole. "I heard we may be eligible for resentencing," he says. "Life with a possibility of parole is still life for someone with my record."

A year ago, the Director's Review Board invalidated Eddie's indeterminate segregated housing unit program, concluding that he was no longer a threat to the general population. Eddie's first fifteen years of incarceration had been conducted as a "good homie," meaning someone who could be counted on to hurt or kill those who broke the prison rules or were considered "no good."

Gang affiliated since the age of twelve – dropping out of school at age fourteen, dying from a bullet to the chest only to be revived by a surgeon's hands – he props up like a cobra as we take a stroll around the track under a summer morning in the high desert of Lancaster State Prison.

I met Eddie a few years ago at another prison: young and indoctrinated into the prison culture, ripped with muscles and tattoos covering his body and arms, and then there's his stare, intimidating but with a face as smooth as a baby's. I befriended Eddie, as a peer and as someone with a similar background, but I was taken aback by how different our paths were headed.

We take a seat at one of the concrete tables facing a group of prisoners chasing after a soccer ball. While pigeons flock around the table, we watch their necks breaking for crumbs. Eddie who has a surgical scar running down the middle of his torso, smiles lightly as he coos at the birds. I imagine myself flying above, eyeing the horizon, taking in the shifting winds, looking down on Edie at the table. He rubs his fingers, and a pigeon flies into his hand. He raises the flapping bird to his face, perks his lips, and feeds the avian from his mouth.

Then I remember why Eddie is different from other prisoners. It is Eddie who reminds me of Viktor Frankl's words: "Any man can, even under such circumstances, decide what shall become of him – mentally and spiritually."* Kneeling on the grass, he embodies the image of a mother eagle feeding her chicks: tenderly, methodically, flicking mince dry bundles of bread into their beaks.

Eddie's change was subtle and hard to discern from the stereotypes with whom I'd hardly interacted. We had nothing in common: not in aspirations, nor business, but Eddie and I had a history and learned to relate through our passion for books and poetry, pull-ups and soccer, and an eclectic taste in music. Over the year, I have suggested that Eddie take college courses. His re-sentencing and plausible release has been on my mind. I imagine him standing before a judge, pleading why he deserves a second chance.

What is it about sitting in prison for life that reflects a fight for hope that causes one's thoughts to hold on to that vision of freedom? I see it in the youthfulness mirrored in the eyes of an aging face. I see it in the desire of a heart learning to exist with a fleeting image of a parent's, a wife's, or a child's affection. Eddie, crouched on the floor, reminds me of a man willing to fight for hope. He walks back to the table and asks, in an inquisitive voice, "Are you ready for resentencing?" I am not sure whether to answer as the person I have become, or for my potential as a man, so I pause and share a thought, quoting from C.S. Lewis: "When a man has been perverted from his youth and taught that cruelty is the right thing, does some tiny little kindness, perhaps, risk being sneered at by his companions, he may, in God's eyes, be doing more than you and I would do if we gave up life for a friend" Then Eddie asks, T-shirt in hand, "Do you think I have a chance?"

A black raven swoops out of nowhere, an ominous stillness flapping between us, and lands like a dark cloud on the grass. Eddie turns and looks me in the eyes, and shakes his head, extinguishing his already fragile state of hope.

What is he thinking? Or trying to decipher? His expression is so down cast, his face shadows in the midst of an overcast morning. Can belief in something – or desiring fate take its course – count as fighting for it?

I stare toward the sky, gray and spacious, its gloom reflected on the yard, a biting wind slapping in from the east, debris swirling from the ground in bundles. We sit still beneath its shadow, the notice of the yard distancing, recreation turning from activity to passivity.

"They'll never release me," he utters, "I have stabbed too many people."

"But you've changed!" I sit up and scan his face, wanting to see a glimpse of hope, but there is none.

"How I wish I had your faith."

His voice falling, surrendering to a system that has claimed so many in ways I can't understand. Eddie pulls his T-shirt over his head.

The next day, I make my way to poetry class. I slide into a back corner chair, and begin reading a piece written by one of the prisoners. After I'm done, I pinch my pen and roll it across a white blank paper and stare at the faceless words. Still seeking inspiration, I slip out and take a walk through a starlit night. Above the gun tower, the moon hangs over and sneaks around the table where Eddie and I sat talking about our possibilities of going home one day. Lancaster Prison is located in Los Angeles County, only an hour drive from where I grew up. A lot of people I know live close by. I imagine them sitting on their couch, tummies full, lounging in front of a 36-inch flat screen, happy, and watching as a family.

I was born in Los Angeles in 1973. I was raised among the gang infested *barrios* and disenchanted street corners. My role models were these baggy-clothed *cholos* that patrolled the neighborhood day and night. At age seventeen, I had no goals and no plans for the future; I lived in the moment, and acted impulsively, smoking weed and skipping school. Bent on proving myself, I, with homeboys from my street gang, decided to rob a man who was returning home. We robbed and killed him, with no reason but to take his money, trying to be someone that I wasn't. Now I spend long hours in a prison cell, atop a steel bunk and a million thoughts, wishing I could change the past and undo my gang affiliation, and everything leading up to that horrific night.

Hanging on the pull-up bar in the yard, I listen to Eddie's concentrated breathing. I wonder if the same dedication with which he works out with was focused on regaining his freedom, he'd be strong enough to conquer his pessimism. I see a prisoner walk up and shake his hand, who sometimes distracts him with prison chatter, disrupting, gossiping about what other prisoners are doing or not doing.

Eddie sometimes gets caught up in what he's done and where he's been, even when he hates when others do it. He turns to me, as if we had a prior engagement, "You ready?" and signals me to walk around the yard.

At work, a week ago, during lunch break, I found Eddie sitting like a student taking a test and writing in a note pad; his reading glasses clinging mid-nose. I watched as if I didn't know him, his gaze fixed on what seemed a moment of inspiration. I sat across from him, hoping he would look up, but he was intent on writing, so I said, "Eddie!"

He looked up and broke into a smile, "I'm writing some thoughts down, I've been thinking about what you said and I think I'm ready to start believing."

I got up and joined him at the table.

In attempting to motivate Eddie, I encouraged him to take more self-help classes. To ease his nerves, I outlined a plan: take two classes per week, anger management and conflict resolution, Narcotics Anonymous/Alcoholics Anonymous on Saturdays, and the last four days you can split between your workouts and poetry class. After you complete those two, you can start on parenting and victim awareness classes, and perhaps, take a college course? But Eddie's fidgeting told me to back away from the college courses.

After I've drawn a modest plan around his weekly schedule, allowing him to keep most days of his routine in tack, Eddie proposes that I join him in some of the classes. I agree and tell him that is an excellent idea.

On our first day of anger management the instructor begins by asking each student for his name and to briefly explain why he's in the class. I notice a sign of panic in Eddie's face as his turn approaches. He shifts in his seat and runs his palms down his pant legs. I reach out and tap his shoulder from the back seat, *no pasa nada"* (there's nothing to worry about).

Then I see a sign of confidence: his hands lock together atop the desk, his posture unbends, and I notice a tone that points to a man who is ready.

"My name is Eddie Gonzalez, and I am here today to learn how to manage my anger, a problem that has gotten me into a lot of trouble."

Eddie, the former "good-homie," prison enforcer, always marching to the beat of the prison rules, lays down his pride and embraces his true self. And then, with the redeeming quality I have seen within him, he is present and in minutes he is participating, jotting down every word in his note pad.

When the reality of his potential became clear to him, Eddie experienced a new struggle within himself. His reputation, what he did to further his street gang and his name in prison, suddenly begins to weigh on him. His new-found conscience relegated him to his cell, which he swore he hated after spending eight years in isolation. So he knew how this could affect him – at least I want to believe he did. I often wonder if he is scared to go out into a new world, not knowing what to expect, how to survive? He's told me that he can't see himself getting a job with all the tattoos he has.

Not seeing him out on the yard or in class, I enter the housing unit and go straight toward Eddie's cell. The cell is cave dark, emanating what light it can from the 13-inch television. On the lower bunk, I can barely make out a body in a fetal position. Eddie lying under both covers and darkness, with his face toward the wall. Rumor was that he's been loaded on heroine. One glace and it's clear that Eddie is slipping, diminishing any notion of rehabilitation, as if he might be sinking down into a quicksand of blinding darkness. I don't understand exactly why progress and change became such a complicated task for lifers with a possibility of freedom: you need to change, you need to educate yourself, learn why you committed your crime, and seek to mature into a productive person. I can't imagine myself wanting to spend the rest of my life in prison; apathy runs like a disease in here. And I, like many prisoners, am guilty of concealing my frustration. We just go through the daily routines as if nothing affects us, merely existing, crippled by the fear of actually making a difference.

I want to knock on Eddie's cell door to wake him, but the situation feels too somber for such an interruption. Besides, he needs to crawl out of this hole alone. The power to change lies within. Change the thought process, a news person will arise.

Parting from Eddie's cell, I see familiar faces: young, middle-aged, and old prisoners, reminding me of how my youthfulness will continue to decline incrementally.

In the early years of my imprisonment, I had no idea if a sentence of life without the possibility of parole could ever change, or if it was even possible. I told myself, if I'm gonna die in here, I will go out my way − exercise and reading has carried me along. But one day the law changed for me and now I'm eligible to have a possibility, a real chance, to regain my freedom. This unexpected miracle appeared just when I began to have serious doubts whether the law could ever change.

Out in the yard, I look for someone to talk with, but my confidants are all engaged in activities. One is playing soccer, another is at work, a third is playing chess. Finally, I see Eddie stepping out of the building.

He squints as the light exposes his sickness, but he mans-up and heads in my direction. He can read my facial expression, see my body language. For all his shortcomings, it's astounding how he owns his demons. Part of it, of course, is that he has always been transparent, but part must be from his subconscious desire for change, to become a decent human being. Spiritually, I am feeling that emotional honesty, the way one feels upon granting forgiveness.

He is sick and wants to sit. I lead him to a grassy patch, next to a towering night light, and we sit. A lively chorus plays around us in A-minor: sparrows chirping, pigeons cooing, ravens barreling staccato percussions, the hallow wind of the valley blows from unknown distance. His pale face is accentuated from the light. Then looking away, he says: "I've been fucking up."

Disappointment hangs from my face, my mind and heart feel like an encounter of unreconciled lovers. My lungs need oxygen, my tongue knotted dry. Maybe it's the failed expectation of wanting too much for Eddie or the missing satisfaction found in being part of his change, but most likely it's my impatience. I feel defeated. I look away, lower my head, pull out a hand full of grass and try to feel indifferent. I imagine shaking my hand in disapproval and parting ways, content that at least I had tried to help, but I cannot.

As I struggle to refrain from saying something I will regret, a mental picture comes to me. A recurring dream I often have when I'm about to fall asleep: I am reclining outside in a lush-green back yard at home. It's summer. A perfect day at the pool. I'm watching two brown-haired children swimming in the Caribbean blue waters, jumping in and screaming with joy. I'm there with the love of my life, the mother of my children, enjoying a blissful afternoon with the people I love most. This is a reality I wish for Eddie to experience. I try to see it now, but the Eddie before me cannot be seen in this serene picture.

Eddie sits motionless, as if his body has lapsed into rigor mortis. "I'm done getting loaded," he says, noticing my inattention.

"For good!" he blurts out, with an unfamiliar tone. *"Ya estuve con ese madre*! (I'm done with that shit!)."

"I'm looking at things differently," he continues. I'm sorry. You've been a good *camarada* (friend).

I tell him how disappointed I am. He says he knows and understands if I want to cut him loose, he'll figure this out.

"I got you." I say. "Get up, let's roll out." I grab his hand and lift him to his feet. It's yard recall and we must go back to our cells.

As we make our way to the housing unit, I stir him to take the long way around the track. The sun breaking through the clouds, lighting the valley and the mountains beyond, it's only Eddie and I walking toward our housing unit. Slowly we enter the sally port and wait for the gate to open.

Eddie leans back against the wall and squares in front of me, pulls his hand out of his pocket – extends his fingers, and shakes my hand. I look straight into his eyes, nodding my head in approval. He leans forward and embraces me as if he were drawing all the people he has hurt into his arms.

The gate opens and together we enter the unit and head toward our separate cells.

Quotes:

C.S. Lewis, Mere Christianity," p. 91
Viktor Frankl, *Man's Search for Meaning*

Joel went before the Board of Parole Hearing and proved that he has successfully transformed his life. He was released in December of 2015 and is currently attending college and working for the Anti-Recidivism Coalition in Los Angeles.

ADAGE

"To err is human, to forgive is divine."

From Dumb to Dumber

BY DORTELL WILLIAMS

They say, the more you learn, the dumber you realize you are. Over the past two decades of incarceration, this refrain has followed me like a sour odor. Early on, I began my education with great difficulty. I struggled in reading and math, being elevated from grade to grade, almost automatically. Yet with each grade level, I sank in confidence. I saw absolutely no purpose in history; the past was the past. I often responded in rebellion. Home economics was for girls, my simplistic view, with several layers of chauvinistic bias intertwined. In reality, I was lost in a haze of academic confusion with no help or hope in sight. I believed I had simply fallen too far behind.

Yet, for the love of my dear mother, I accomplished just enough to graduate. In 1994, she proudly witnessed me walk across the stage with my peers – accepting a diploma that was diluted by a 2.85 GPA. I was as ill-prepared for life as anyone ever could be.

I approach my counselor the year prior to graduation, seeking to fill a curiosity more than anything else. To my surprise, I was flat out told I "wasn't college material." I wasn't encouraged to try. I wasn't viewed as one with any potential. However, I did have street smarts, or so I believed. After graduation, I simply threw myself down into the short, dark, twisted slide of the underworld. I adopted the life of drug dealing, looking for an easy way through life.

The world of criminality is a universe of its own. The sub-culture of violence and self-centeredness. The fatalistic views: The "me against the world" attitude. The "win at all costs" mindset. I bit into them all. Before I knew it, the lure of fast money, the illusion of a long, successful life in crime – the money, the attention of women, the shiny cars and jewelry – all fed my faulty thinking. It was a lifestyle I chose, a lifestyle that hardened and calloused me to the core.

I lived that life, without incident, save for one speeding ticket, for five years. During that time, I learned to network; I met all types of people – from both worlds: gangsters, bankers, car thieves, drug financiers and a lot of functional addicts. I got jobs in retail management to justify my income, eventually starting a commercial landscaping business to wash money through. To my surprise, I was learning and excelling more on my own than I had in school. The experiences gave re-birth to my confidence. A confidence that turned to arrogance, an impenetrable self-will and the next thing I knew, my house of cards was blown away by the first real wind against it. I was convicted of murder at the age of twenty-three, sentenced to life without the possibility of parole. I was deemed incorrigible

The tension on Pelican Bay's Facility-A was as thick as marsh humidity, only colder, much colder. Within seconds, the morning exercise period metastasized into a fierce battle between two vicious prison gangs. Fists flew and makeshift knives sliced. As I stood by, mouth dry, my heart thumping like a hollow drum, I was awash in numbness.

The gun guard's deafening shouts to "get down!" reverberated between the cinder block row of eight housing units on the yard. Only his 9mm shots – one warning into the air and the following blast directly into the melee – were more punishing. A lethal shot splintered the crowd of combatants, revealing one young, blood-ridden prisoner slumped on the ground, his lower jaw ghastly eviscerated.

As barbaric as it all sounds, this is your contemporary California Department of Corrections and Rehabilitation, where violent incidents like this are all too common. It's almost predictable, as programs and activities are erased, the violence grows more savage.

When the tools for cognitive development are stripped, people become nothing more than instinctual beings motivated by fear and self-centered survival. The ignorant are forced to rely on their deepest primal impulses; the strongest and the fittest rule the jungle, and in here, it's the prison cliques, which increase in number as men mask their fear and join the ranks.

Meanwhile, for fifteen years I searched for a positive distraction from the daily, brutal madness that always seemed too close and inevitably contagious, no matter how hard I resisted. I wrote CDC headquarters and suggested a program based on personal, individual behavior. The response was not favorable.

A disciplinary-free record at Pelican Bay earned me a transfer closer to home in southern California, where I could at least get visits. Some two days later, after a nine-hundred mile bus ride, accommodated by dry peanut butter sandwiches – for breakfast, lunch and dinner, and fettered from my hips to my feet – my destination was the state prison at Calipatria. Drained and exhausted, I was immune to the rancid-smelling holding cell – grimy bars, sticky floors and all. When I was finally attended, I was told that the entire prison, each of the four separate facilities, were on restriction due to an institutional war between two rival factions. My orientation to Calipatria consisted of a three-month lockdown. Other than the visits, my new concrete home was nothing but more of the same: bloody, violent, and traumatic.

Once settled, I was still eager to learn what other potential resides within me after my short-lived run as an "entrepreneur." Yet there was very little opportunity for self-betterment in my new maximum-security home. The only thing I learned was that prison is a lawless place for lawless people.

Despite all of the chaos, I was still able to earn a paralegal certificate through correspondence. Some generous and able friends footed the bill and their investment in me paid off. I completed the course with a 96 percent GPA, and honors. It was my first major accomplishment. My appetite for knowledge only grew, but remained unfulfilled for some time to come.

Finally, in 2003, by pure serendipity, I was transferred to the state prison in Los Angeles County, situated approximately ninety minutes east of Los Angeles – nearly fifteen years later. It was at this time that I was introduced to what they called, The Honor Program.

After enduring years of mind-numbing idleness, excruciating boredom and chain-linked ignorance, the many programs at the Honor Program were a welcomed privilege. One of the first classes I took was creative writing, taught by fellow prisoner Kenneth E. Hartman, a giant of a man with a commanding voice just as large. Harman showed me how to structure my essays and the many particulars of the publishing industry. His tutelage gave me a new path toward self-efficacy. A year or so later, when Harman moved on to other projects, I was approached by the chairman of the Men For Honor Inmate Leisure Time Activity Group, Macio Lindsey. Medium-build with a walnut complexion, and a slight afro, Lindsey asked me to teach a writing class. I was all too thrilled to accept the challenge. By then I had established myself as a published writer.

Still, I think the most valuable lesson for me in Hartman's creative writing class was being forced to read aloud. I had never read aloud before. In fact, it wasn't until I came to prison that I'd ever read an entire book. These experiences awakened my interest in academics and gave me a new zeal for confronting my scholastic deficiencies.

In the interim, I took a conflict resolution class, offered through Friends Outside, an independent self-help organization that CDCR allows to provide classes. This class not only helped me realize that I harbored a lot of anger and resentment, but also gave me a host of coping skills to confront these issues.

I also signed up for critical thinking, taught by a fellow prisoner named Amir. Tall with a shiny dome, he taught with conviction and authority. My first assignment was to offer an argument -- in front of the class – on my opposition to the death penalty. Since I had faced death row, I had no problem expressing opposition to it. My presentation was applauded and I felt an enormous sense of accomplishment, especially for being able to speak before an audience without succumbing to nerves.

However, little did I know, my assignment wasn't over. I was then assigned to make a presentation supporting the death penalty. It was a serious challenge. This exercise helped me deal with personal bias, expanded my views and taught me how to be more objective. I nailed it! My nerves no longer betrayed me when speaking before an audience; my nervousness simply melted away. Thinking beyond myself helped me navigate through the mainstream lens. Funny, I had not so much as heard of critical thinking in high school, and here I was learning it in prison – from other prisoners!

Prior to prison, my worldview was very narrow. There were times when I would get into shootouts with other drug dealers over choice locations. At some point during my various reading, I learned that Wall Street exchanges over seven trillion dollars a day. I was astounded. And here we were shooting at one another for criminal crumbs. When I taught creative writing, I explained that observation, and I expounded on how difficult it is to step on each other's toes, particularly if we widen our worldview. I further explained that there are so many magazines, newspapers, and other mediums, that everyone of us, in a single class, or an entire facility, could see the same incident, and each of us could write about it, in our own unique style or genre. Almost any incident can be conveyed in poetical, satirical or lyrical form. There is enough room in the world for us all. I believe that this is a very important lesson because many of us are, or were, extremely territorial.

My worldview grew even larger when I learned the concept of making amends. I owe this lesson to Raymond Dentley, who successfully paroled in 2012, after instructing the Lifer class. Dentley taught me the concept of making amends. Dentley, tall, brown-skinned with black-framed glasses, taught me that there are three types of amends: 1. Direct amends, where one gives back directly to the victim, if possible, 2. Indirect amends, where one gives back in general, and, 3. Life-long amends, where one shows a long-term pattern of giving back and helping others.

With Dentley's encouragement, I suggested we incorporate the Caring For Others Project, under the umbrella of Men For Honor. Through CFO, we collect voluntary funds from our participants – which range from 90 to 150 guys. The collection period endures for three months, for a charity chosen by majority vote. We then donate the total.

Following Dentley's release, Donald Moss, short with black, square-framed glasses, and Quentin Shorter, a vibrant, nitty-gritty old soul, brought twenty-five years, respectively, of prison experience to the Lifer class. Through their own experience, a litany of mistakes were spelled out before an attentive class as cautionary tales. Effective communication skills, good study habits and emotional intelligence pointers were wholly digested by the class. Moss and Shorter put a shine on self-help and to this day, the writing list for the Lifer's class continues to grow.

Due to the proliferation of inactive gang members here on the Honor Yard, Donald Green approached me with an idea to confront that issue. Coming in with excellent preparation skills, Green had already written Criminal Gang Members Anonymous, Inc. in Los Angeles, and obtained permission to use their curricula as a basis for what became the Men For Honor New Choices, Different Directions class. It was around this time that the official name of this facility was changed to the Progressive Programming Facility. Like all PPF classes, the waiting list for New Choices is longer than can be accommodated with a single class. (Green's story can be found on p.171.)

The creative writing class also revealed to me how important reading is. So I aimed to construct the Men For Honor Library — one book donation at a time. The Men For Honor Library now has over seventy-five titles available, ranging from fiction to academic and just about everything in between.

Friends Outside also offered a thought-provoking parenting class. Sadly, my daughter was a precious two-year-old when I was sent to prison. I've been buried within these walls ever since. She is now a twenty-eight-year-old woman. Nevertheless, I had an open mind, I took the class for the experience. What I learned is that there are a number of right ways to raise a child. There are techniques I had never ever considered. I now recommend parenting for everyone, even those without children. Parenting helped me foster healthy relationships with my nieces and nephews, the children of friends, and now, the many children I mentor through organizations Men For Honor partners with. Unfortunately, Friends Outside no longer provides classes for this facility.

Reformers Unanimous, headquartered in Illinois, is an extremely helpful addictions course that introduced biblically-based approaches to overcoming detrimental habits and destructive addictions that fuel failure. RU also fostered a brotherhood of trust and accountability. The Catalyst Foundation, centered right here in Lancaster, gave me insight on my past traumas, how to deal with those traumas, while recognizing them in others. Catalyst is taught by Dave Mashore, who has volunteered to teach on a weekly basis since 2006. It was in this class that I learned what empathy is, and how it can be a useful tool in dealing with others when they act out negatively towards me. Learning not to internalize the drama of others has made my life a lot less stressful.

The Paving the Way Foundation, which is also based in Lancaster, offers a class, taught by Janie Hodge, another deeply appreciated volunteer. In short, this class is a relationship course. Like parenting, Paving the Way delves into family dysfunction and how to deal with personal attitudinal issues such as anger, resentment, abuse and control. Many of us, this writer included, were so acclimated to family dysfunction, we viewed it as normal, which makes it likely to endure generationally. Paving the Way helped me recognize what is and what is not healthy in all relationships.

In the interim, while taking these and related self-help correspondence courses, an odd transformation took place within Men For Honor. All three of its former executive body members transferred within the span of a few months. Macio Lindsey was shipped to Calipatria. Danny Segovia was transferred to the California Men's Colony, a lower-lever institution, and Gregory Valentine volunteered for another facility. I was left alone with a fledgling group that had huge potential, but no long-term direction or purpose. I decided to revive the group by inviting Demetrius Walton, Lester Polk and Doug Porter to restructure Men For Honor and its aims.

As chairman, I was able to expand the array of classes offered by Men For Honor, and gain vital experience by composing various curriculum for many of our new subjects. Nevertheless, in an effort to give others some of the experience I had garnered, and build a well-rounded executive body, I encouraged a lot of position shuffling. I trained Walton to be chairman, and passed the creative writing baton to Polk, giving them a shot at the valuable experience I had already earned. By 2011, we had restructured the group into a full-fledged academic group. Men For Honor was now offering culture through film studies. The aim of creative writing had expanded from teaching basic writing to the additional goal of producing published writers. To date we have nearly forty published writers. In the past eight years, I have had the privilege of absorbing experience in every executive body position: chairman, secretary, treasurer, coordinator and now, the current community advocate.

Polk conducts a component of insight reflection as a part of the writing curricula, which requires creative writing students to complete at least ten hours of reflection on the harm they caused or the reasons why acts were committed in the first place. Polk, tall, dark with an eclectic personality, is also credited with the idea of the Men For Honor Annual Writing Contests, now in its third year. The contests are open to the entire facility, not just Men For Honor participants. The contests offer opportunities in various genres: poetry, screenplays, memoirs and essays. Reflective essays are encouraged. The winners earn a prize, such as sodas paid for out of the Men For Honor account. For some participants, the win is a milestone. Perhaps their first win at anything. Or their first attempt at writing; the first major accomplishment for some. Yet we're all winners in solidarity, mutual support and common good; social jewels scarcely found at other institutions.

Porter, the man we call "Coach," due to his wrestling history as an instructor, is like the wise old owl of the yard. Porter is the father-figure many of us never had. And this is why he was perfect to instruct the Men For Honor Parenting class. As instructor, Porter brings an assuring authority and successful experience with his own eight kids. His question and answer periods, and his unique farm animal analogies liven up the class, and make each cycle a memorable experience.

In addition to allowing me to experience every facet of the group, my years here have allowed me to complete my studies in theology, and eventually earn my doctorate in the field. I have also earned an Associate of Arts degree in Behavioral and Social Science, making the dean's list along the way. In both endeavors, my grade percentage averaged 90-plus. It appears that I was college material after all. I just needed a little guidance and direction.

The Lifer's class continues to help prisoners deal with the hopeless prospects of a life sentence. On the other hand, it proved counter-productive that some of the correctional officers accused the Lifer group of trying to manipulate the Board of Parole Hearings. They figured that since we focused on subjects such as overcoming triggers, understanding empathy and insight, tracing individual causative factors of criminal behavior, and successful interview techniques, we were cheating, coaching to get past the Board.

From our perspective, the BPH's requirements had always been a mystery, which increased the likelihood of failure. With the help of lawyers, we learned the mechanics of BPH preparation, which was recently validated through a former student's Board transcripts. The Board panel praised Vantrea Gregory for addressing these issues prior to his hearing and being wholly prepared. They also praised Gregory for having documentation that he had completed a mock board hearing. He was found suitable and released. (See Gregory's testimony at p. 168.)

Others opposed our self-help in general, often remarking that the class space, and surveillance of our classes, were a waste for people who would never get out. Then Proposition 36 was passed by the voters, allowing non-violent three-strikers an opportunity to have their cases reviewed. If they were truly non-violent, had shown efforts at self-help and were disciplinary free, they were eligible to file for sentence reductions. It seemed the rewards to volunteerism and paying it forward were never ending.

In addition, in 2013 California Senate Bill 9 passed, opening the door for California prisoners sentenced to life without the possibility of parole as juveniles to earn re-sentencing upon showing remorse and rehabilitation. The requirements for such sentencing reductions are active rehabilitation (the BPH frowns on idleness), documents of remorse, making amends, all of which the Progressive Programming Facility provides. In 2014, Senate Bill 260 passed, allowing for earned reductions in sentencing for juveniles sentenced to both determinate and indeterminate sentences. The requirements are the same as those set forth in Senate Bill 9. To date, three of our participants have successfully had their sentences reduced, with several more pending. Over the past three years, nearly twenty men have been released, who previously had no hope of ever getting a second chance.

In 2013, the Men For Honor experienced another transformation. Walton stepped down as chairman, transferring to another facility. Allen Burnett was invited to lead Men For Honor. Since his involvement, the group has adopted the concept of partnering with outside organizations. The Men For Honor now proudly partners with New Beginning Outreach, which supports the Men For Honor Workforce Development and New Choices, Different Directions classes. New Beginnings also offers transitional housing, and other support for parolees. Burnett, a light-complexioned African-American with Asian eyes, and an ever-smiling face, instructs Workforce Development.

These days I concentrate on instructing the Victim Sensitivity class, and beginner Spanish. The Victim Sensitivity class is fashioned in large part from the curricula of the Victim

Offender Education Group, developed in San Quentin by Rochelle Edwards in 2004. The course focuses on victim impact and community harm, insight into criminal behavior and forgiveness. The class also delves into cycles of abuse, addiction and remorse. Spanish, my second language, picked up in prison, teaches the fundamentals of the language with an emphasis on conversation. In addition, cultural understanding and commonality are underscored. Each cycle is met by an enthusiastic group, ready to learn and mutually respectful.

Men For Honor's Personal Development class is met with the same enthusiasm. Jarret Harper, a very tall man with auburn skin and hair, is credited with teaching this class, which focuses on social etiquette: sensitivity to others, harmful idiosyncrasies, argumentative dispositions and negative body language. Harper was also a juvenile when arrested. This class is based on the course, "Character Education," offered by Brigham Young University. In fact, Robert Chan, who previously served as Men For Honor Director, brought more credibility to our courses by suggesting that we base them on actual college courses. Chan, a diminutive American with Chinese heritage and black-framed glasses, is also credited with introducing the Men For Honor In-cell Victimology course, an intense course that is supervised by staff, and based on the curricula of the same name from Colorado State University, Pueblo.

We also partner with Prison Letters 4 Our Struggling Youth, which facilitates our letters of guidance and admonishment to at-risk youth. According to our on-site peer facilitator, Jamon Carr, also a juvenile when he entered the system, we have approximately fifty-four participants involved and growing. The Partnerships for Re-Entry Program, headed by Sister Mary Sean Hodges, helps men on both sides of the walls. For prisoners, PREP offers a number of self-help subjects, which are facilitated through Men For Honor, such as anger management, domestic violence, parenting and life skills. PREP also offers transitional housing once prisoners are paroled, to increase their likelihood of success. PREP is facilitated on the inside by our peer instructor, Lorenzo Flores, who also leads PREP's Victim Empathy module in Spanish.

Clifton Gibson and Joel Aguilar were also invited to the Men For Honor executive body. Gibson, an articulate, muscled young man, and Aguilar, an intelligent, straight-forward man with a very logical viewpoint., brought Helping Y.O.U.T.H. (Youth Offenders Understanding Their Harm). Both were juveniles when arrested over two decades ago. Gibson and Aguilar have a respectable command on insight and causative factors, and co-teach the other twenty-five or so juvenile offenders on the facility. Their methods, and the overall approach of the Men For Honor, were affirmed by a visit from Human Rights Watch lawyer Elizabeth Calvin, who actively encouraged the passing of Senate Bill 9. Through mock trial hearings and intense question and answer sessions of participants, Calvin, Efty Sharoni and Susan Herbert of Loyola Law School, along with Heidi Rummel of the University of California, were all impressed with the growth and maturity of our participants.

It was during this visit that Calvin asked us to write letters to the state legislature to assist her in the passage of Senate Bill 1276. This bill mandates the CDCR to send young offenders to the PPF, and other programming oriented facilitates, as opposed to the war zones many of us started in. Calvin requested that we simply tell our stories; stories such as those included in this book, to convince the legislators to pass this bill. It is difficult to describe our collective joy and satisfaction upon learning that the bill had passed. Many of us have experienced first-hand that war zones are traumatic and a huge distraction from the goal of self-betterment and rehabilitation. We are over joyed that the legislators understood the importance of the passage of SB 1276. And once again, I see those new, valuable parenting skills coming into play.

This isn't to say that the PPF is some prison utopia. There are human beings here, and human beings still err, no matter where you find them. Like any sports club, testosterone sometimes gets the best of men and fists fly. There has been contraband found on the PPF – just like there was in the concentration camps, Jewish holocaust hideouts and other places of deprivation. However, these occurrences are a lot less frequent than any institution I've previously experienced.

Since my arrival here at the PPF, twelve years ago, I have made it a point to waste no time. I have grown spiritually, physically and academically. While I have made my share of bad decisions, I have learned to forgive myself, I have learned that helping others has a healing affect, and that redemption is a worthy chase, even if I, myself, never get freedom.

Over the past two decades, none of these courses or activities were even remotely imaginable at other California institutions. The PPF is a God-send, as are the men on it. Yet, without the support of most custody, and auxiliary staff, none of this would be possible. Meanwhile I'm on a mission to learn all that I can, because the more I learn, the dumber I realize I was. In fact, I think I was a straight idiot!

Sources:
Board of Parole Hearings, RE: Vantrae Gregory. Brian

Wooldridge, Deputy District Attorney, August 27, 2014, pp. 69-70

California Department of Corrections and Rehabilitation, www.cdcr.ca.gov

Faucet, Richard, "Honor Program Success," *Los Angeles Times*, 2003

Madrid v. Gomez, Federal District Court, 2005 (Federal ruling and prohibitions against Pelican Bay State Prison)

Padgett, Julian, *San Quentin News*, "Rochelle Edwards Transitions Out of VOEG's Leadership Role," August 2014, p. 2

Widdison, Marisa, "Bodies Imprisoned, Minds Go Free," *Antelope Valley Press,* October 7, 2006

Pell, C. (1994) "Yes: Pell Grants Dramatically Reduce Recidivism," *USA Today*, March 17, 1994

Taylor, Jon, M. (2008), "Pell Grants for Prisoners: Why Should We Care?"

Taylor, Jon, M. (2004), "Piercing Together a College Education Behind Bars," *Journal of Prisoners on Prison,* Vol. 13, pp. 74-91

Dortell Williams is currently pursuing a BA in Communication Studies, majoring organizational communications at Cal State University -- Los Angeles. He has dedicated his life to rehabilitating himself, earning several academic degrees, including a doctorate in theological studies. He also enjoys mentoring youth and helping others.

A Meeting for Forgiveness

BY LESTER POLK

The drab gray walls amplified the overwhelming sense of enclosure. As I sat in the foyer of the prison visiting room, I knew that this day would be as far from "normal" as any other day I had ever experienced in prison. This was the day I stopped being afraid; the day I stopped running from the wretched past. With the mask of a tough guy, I had always prided myself on my fearlessness; a very broad fearlessness, except what awaited me on the other side of that visiting room door.

Some years after having been involved in a horrible murder, I wrote an apology letter to the victims' family through the district attorney's office. The DA's Office forwarded my letter directly to my victims. To my utter surprise, years later I received a response from the widow of my victim, Ms. Ashley Henderson. * Ms. Henderson described her loss, expressed her concern for my growth and invited me to correspond. I was dumbfounded, but I did respond to her invitation. After a few letters, Ms. Henderson shared her desire to meet me through the Victim Offender Dialogue Program. Of course, I agreed to this. Ms. Leslie Davenport, our mediator visited with me several times prior to what I call the "The Meeting," to explain the process, lay down the rules and get a feel for me as a person.

"Hello Lester," whispered Ms. Davenport, in a very soft, raspy voice. Dressed in a beige, knee-length conservative dress, the somewhat older woman, who spoke with a slightly mid-western accent, shook my hand and went on to prepare me for what would transpire during the meeting. I listened carefully, until my own racing thoughts interrupted my concentration, *Man, can I do this? Do I really have the strength? Could I actually go through with this?* I wiped my sweaty palms across my "Prisoner" stenciled pants as Ms. Davenport continued to read "...and you hereby release to the Department of Corrections any injury or liability arising from this meeting." My heart raced. My mind raced.

"Man, they sure are covering themselves, aren't they?" I uttered.

"Well Lester," she continued, "This process is new. The concepts of forgiveness and understanding are foreign to the correctional system." She loosened up, "It's almost comedic when one considers their name, The Department of Corrections and Rehabilitation," she said with a dry chuckle. Her soft, feminine voice calmed my nerves, though a residual of persistent concern lingered on.

This "mediator" was the exact opposite of myself. Ms. Davenport was small, petite, demure and Caucasian. I am a six-foot-one, two hundred and fifty pound, Black prisoner, deeply ensnared in the clutches of the Criminal Justice System;

perpetually stamped as violent and dangerous. Ms. Davenport saw through the veneer, though. She was quickly able to perceive my fear, anxiety and nervous anticipation. Those were the aspects of my being that she concentrated on. Ms. Davenport saw beyond the cold written record of my past, and viewed the present softer, gentler man who was racked by decades of guilt and shame for a horrific past, now aching to make some type of amends.

From the very first meeting, Ms. Davenport presented herself as a kind, forgiving, trustworthy human being. I had had numerous meetings with her, embraced by the empathetic energy that she so generously provided. From those meetings I learned of the deep damage I had wrought in the lives of my victim's next of kin. I saw no reason to distrust her. After all, she had worked tirelessly to get through the governmental red tape in order to facilitate this meeting. I whispered to myself that I owed Ms. Davenport, and myself, this unique opportunity to experience a very rare restorative justice meeting, as opposed to the ever-unforgiving model of vindictive retribution and endless punishment.

This restorative process was foreign to my way of thinking. As a prisoner, I had been all but tucked away and forgotten. My life had been relegated to four very close walls dotted with locks all about, and not a light to be seen in the foreseeable future—if ever. I had come to like my life as I had painstakingly formed it. It didn't matter, nor did anything else, except for my God and the hereafter. I had my daily routine. I was at least on a peaceful yard, the Progressive Programming Facility, where I could do my own time and be left alone.

I really had no need, or wish, for any reminders of my crime; the greatest shame of my life. But Ms. Davenport had been persistent, even a bit pushy. So I agreed, and began to mentally prepare for the meeting. While I never expected such an opportunity, I had spent many hours involved in group and individual therapy.

One of my favorites was the 24-week Lifer's Therapy class, given by a licensed psychologist. The intense class helped me confront anger issues, personal prejudices and helped me change my delinquent thinking. The psychologist was very accommodating, helping me understand other issues unrelated to the "normal" aberrant thinking. That class gave me a life-long foundation for dealing with issues that had plagued me most of my life.

I was about as ready as I was going to be. After all of the legal preambles, Ms. Davenport took my hand and said, "Okay Lester, were going in there now. Remember to let me know if you would like a break, or if it becomes too intense for you." She reassured me with unmistakable kindness—in voice and manner.

I had come to the visiting room many times before, but it had always been with someone who I was friendly and familiar with. This time I was walking straight towards the gripping fear I had been running from for the past twenty years.

As I sat down, I realized that both, my therapist and my victim's widow, Ms. Henderson, were standing directly in front of me. While I sat there motionless, barraged by a torment of emotions, the most unusual thing occurred. Ms. Henderson held out her hand to me, insisting that we shake hands before we began our meeting. Her impromptu gesture took me by total surprise. I considered the harsh and unforgiving attitude so visibly (and understandably) displayed towards me during my trial. I obliged, hesitantly. My troubled mind was eased a bit by her gesture.

Actually, my story does not start here; it starts nearly two decades ago, way before I became inmate #H-72800. At that time Ms. Henderson had been blessed with life as a wife, mother and a youth counselor involved in juvenile diversion programs. She was a compassionate giver, a pro-social citizen. I was a misguided, insensible youth—mainly by choice.

I was full of ignorance and unresolved anger issues. I had agreed to participate in a robbery that resulted in the premature death of Mrs. Henderson's husband, Frank Henderson. If that wasn't' enough, I was deemed to be the sole agitator, who acted with what the Justice System terms, "Reckless indifference to human life." I see that now. I agree with this description, but this wasn't the Lester Polk that those close to me were familiar with. The criminal Polk was a foreign avatar *I* didn't even recognize. This delinquent Polk was a perversion, the anti-thesis to my true character. Every time I think about the Polk I should have been, the Polk I had the potential to be, the reality of the act I committed shattered those expectations. Imagine being hunted by the very person you have to live with, and see in the mirror, every single day of your life—minute by minute, day by day, through the decades. There was a time in my life when I was considered one of the most promising, rising stars in my family. There were clear and reasonable expectations placed before me for my future. I was expected to earn a college degree, a military commission, and create and raise a family. My fate had been written in the hearts and minds of my loving family, but contrary to those noble expectations, stood the conspicuous reality of a life of regret and sorrow. My failure weighs on me like an anvil. This is why when Ms. Henderson offered me her hand to shake, I felt so unworthy.

Once seated, Ms. Davenport reminded us that, "The rules I

explained to you are pretty simple. We will allow each other the opportunity to speak, before interjecting or commenting." We each nodded in agreement.

Ms. Henderson initiated the meeting with a request, her face very serious: "Tell me Mr. Polk, in your own words, the events that led you to be in my bedroom that horrible evening?" Her brown eyes focused intently and expectantly into my eyes. I looked down, noting that her tone was not angry, but instead firm, yet affable. I felt at ease enough to respond—after a long pause.

I then reluctantly began to recount the deadly events that extinguished one life, and marred so many others.

"Well, Ms. Henderson, I was involved with a group of people, not really what I would call friends. I had heard that they were making a great deal of money from robberies. Thoughtless, I only saw the potential money; never did I imagine that things would go so terribly wrong. When I met up with these guys, I told them that I wanted in. I wasn't even originally a part of their crew. I was an outsider, vaguely aware of their activities, but part of the same neighborhood."

Ms. Henderson held that intense eye-to-eye focus, yet clearly disconnected. She could not understand, to any degree, the sub-culture to which I was describing to her. I continued to explain, determined now. Then I explained the randomness in which her house was chosen. She remained silent the entire time. But the moment I explained how her house was chosen she seemed astounded, even angry. "Say that again!" she demanded. "Do you mean to tell me that it was by sheer *chance* that my house was selected?" Shamefully, with my head already lowered, I affirmed. "We were led to believe there was a safe inside that contained thousands of dollars," I added, as if that might help. I explained to Ms. Henderson how their avid denials of having a safe fell on deaf ears. And despite our failure to find a safe, the "rule" was to never leave a robbery empty handed.

Ms. Henderson sat stoically. Those eerie few moments seemed like a life time. Her silence only pronounced my terror and shame, as they returned to haunt me with a vengeance. I felt like a fly caught in an extractable web. I wanted to run and hide, but as I looked to my right, Ms. Davenport offered a reassuring nod.

Following a long silence, I asked Ms. Henderson, "Can I read a letter I wrote to you as part of my therapy? I call it 'Victim Shoes.' I wrote it as if you were writing it to me, about the trauma and devastation that my actions caused." Ms. Henderson agreed, and so I began to read:

"Dear Mr. Polk,

Allow me to introduce myself to you. My name is Ashley Henderson. I am the widow of Mr. Frank Henderson, husband and father to our three children; two beautiful girls and one fine man. He was a successful businessman, community leader and the love of my life. That was the man you stole from my life. Now, I know you didn't "pull the trigger," but I hold you to the same judicial standards as the killer of my love, because, as they say, "in for a penny, in for a pound."

I want you to understand that I am not using this opportunity to place additional guilt in your life, but you need to realize that on June 14, 1991, you stole more than my husband, four thousand dollars, and the innocence of my children. You stole my life. You stole my dreams; my peace of mind. You stole my quiet moments; family gatherings and the list goes on and on.

For weeks, months, years, I had no time to grieve because I

had to bury my husband, attend to my heart broken children and deal with your trial. When I was finally able to grieve, I just wandered around the house like a ghost in a grave yard. I haunted Frank's closet; I opened the drawers and cabinets; I touched his shirts and jackets—burying my face in his clothes, trying to breathe in his scent. Sometimes I would shut myself in our room and hold the last pictures of us together, and weep.

The pain did not start or stop with just me. My daughters, Lisa and Deborah, lost their father, and my son, Eric, never got to meet his father. Deborah had just given birth days after her father's death, so he, Frank, never got a chance to see his grandchild. The child grew up without having the wisdom of a loving grandfather.

Lisa, well, she got hammered with the worst of it. As you already know, Frank died in her arms. The object of her love and safety bled out I front of her. Can you possibly imagine the horrible thoughts that ran through her mind? The utter feelings of hopelessness that stayed with her? So much that she turned to drugs and troubles of all kinds trying to numb the pain.

Don't fool yourself into thinking that those forty-eight horrifying minutes are long gone. For Lisa, whenever she sees a Black man, the tragedy would trigger all over again. The anger, the hate in your voice stayed with her, as well as with me, and still does to this day.

I was a youth activist in a juvenile hall before you and your gang violently entered my life, and even after what you did, I found it to be my life's calling. Especially after I found out that you were all teens.

I hear that you changed your life, and are now serving the

Lord, God. Well, I prayed for that to happen. I am glad that you received forgiveness for your soul. I, too, offer you my forgiveness, which means that I no longer hold you in the context of our tragic meeting. I truly believe you are sorry for what you did. You do have my forgiveness, and simply put, I wrote this letter to let you know what you are forgiven for."

I had used the letter as a shield, holding it close to my face as I read. I didn't feel worthy enough to look Ms. Henderson in her eyes. However, as I lowered my shield, to my surprise, her eyes were filled with tears.

She looked directly at me, tears streaming. As she wiped them away, her chest lifted, her head raised and she announced, "You actually get it! I just wanted to know if you understood. That means so much to me!" She exclaimed.

My mind seemed to dim, numb, but my mouth naturally muttered, "I'm so very sorry. I can only express to you that since that horrifying day, I have spent my life trying to be the exact opposite of the boy who destroyed your life that shameful night."

With a kind of nurturing look on her face, Ms. Henderson said, "We all need forgiveness, Lester. We are all sinners," she said. "If there was something that I could do to earn my right-eousness, then I would not need Jesus. But we all need forgiveness and salvation, Lester. Besides that, I would like to offer you my friendship."

At that my eyes lit up like lanterns. She continued, "I would like for us to get to know one another. I think it would be a Jesus-like ending to this tragedy. Beside, we might as well be friends now, because well be together in heaven for eternity. I truly believe that is what the Lord would want. In this life tragedies happen to us, but it is what we do with them that is the test."

I listened with what must have been a look of bewilderment on my face. Tears rolled down as I sat there confused, absorbing all that Ms. Henderson was saying. Finally, I responded, "Yes, I will be your friend. I consider your friendship a gift from God. I will do my absolute best to be the best friend I can possibly be."

As the meeting continued on, the heaviness I had gone out there with had all but evaporated. The meeting had turned into a visit as we chatted and learned more about one another. It was a new chapter to a twenty-year-old encounter. I spoke of breakthroughs in my therapy, and she shared the triumphs of her children. I shared the insanity of the prison system, and I explained what a blessing it is to be here on this facility, and how this place helped me prepare for my meeting with her.

I told her how violent and crazy the last prison I was at had been. I described the riots, the jackings for canteen, and how prevalent the same mindset that caused me to run in her house was in prison. Ms. Henderson sat silently, sticking to the rule of not interrupting, though all formalities had by now gone out of the window. Ms. Davenport seemed to bask in the success of the meeting and remained a silent observer.

Ms. Henderson shared stories of counter thinking as well. She told me about family members who think our meeting is insane. She confided in me how an acquaintance who was accompanying her at Mass on a recent Sunday chided her for coming to meet me and even considering an olive branch. I laughed inside at the irony. *Perhaps the acquaintance didn't hear Jesus' message on forgiveness,* I thought to myself.

Hours later the institution was cutting short our visit, and all programs for that matter, to conduct an emergency count. As we stood to leave, I offered to shake Ms. Henderson's hand, but she abruptly shoved it to the side, and opened her arms with a smile. She stood there, insisting, until I walked in and let her envelop me. She squeezed me as if I were long-lost family.

As I lined up for in-take into the housing unit, my fellow prisoners commented about my obvious glow. It was evident that something special had occurred because, according to my neighbor, I was "beaming." So I shared my wonderful experience in the briefest version possible. He was amazed, as well as those in earshot.

The usual and collective experiences with victims consist of sometimes hateful, always tear-filled and emotion-driven statements to the court. In contrast, my meeting was a unique, bright, warm light the likes of which are unheard of in the dark, negative, cold world of typical prison. Yet, this is my story, and I intend to be worthy of it.

In the meantime, I will continue to rebuild myself, enroll in therapy, mentor and instruct others, as well as humble myself as a student. And no other facility would be more conducive for such positive growth, than the Progressive Programming Facility.

*All names listed are fictional

Lester Polk is a charter member of the Men For Honor group. He loves God, is creative, and strives to educate himself. He is a seminary school graduate, is a peer-to-peer mentor, and facilitator of a self-help correspondence program called Partnership for Re-entry Program. As part of his commitment to restoration, he has met with the survivors of his crimes and made restitution. Polk strives to model his transformation through living amends and his craft, creative writing. His award winning essays are available at: Medium.com/View-ThroughtheRazorWire/LesterL.Polk

CHINESE PROVERB

"Be not afraid of slow growth, but rather of standing still."

Freedom Train

BY KORY DARTY

I Kory Darty, arrived on the freedom train, here on the Progressive Programming Facility, at Lancaster on February 6, 2012. Radiant spirits greeted me and the vibe of the place was the closest I had seen to normal in a long time. Instead of "where you from?" or "Who you run with?" or even hardened staring faces, I was met with respectful greetings and extended welcomes. It was an amazing and exciting sight to see, with all of the different races interacting and getting along. I could not believe I did not have to ask somebody for "security" to use the yard toilet. On the more volatile spots, you would have to ask someone you trust to stand watch behind you while your back was against the yard and you relieved yourself.

I was captivated every single day during my first weeks here by all the positive programs, self-help classes, and helpful fellow prisoners. Unlike my first two weeks in other prisons where I saw a prisoner lose his life to violence and prison politics. I was at San Quentin, it was on the weight pile, and many white inmates were surrounding a tall, skinny white inmate. The vibe was bad, very bad. I will never forget it. They started fighting and the next thing I knew the victim was on the ground stabbed in his neck. The yard alarm was activated and the yard gunner was yelling for everyone to get down. They were still scuffling when the gunner shot the victim in the neck, aiming for his attackers. It took the medical staff over an hour to remove his body, but his spirit had already been sent into the next life. I will never forget all the blood on the yard, looking at that spot days later where the victim took his last breath.

When I was offered to come here, I had to ponder the nature of prison. I continuously have to discern between the battles I chose to fight, and the war to survive and get out as scheduled I decided to take the road to normalization, not realizing to what level normal could be found here. The PPF gave me a new energy, and the opportunity to grow out of my immaturity and adolescence. My "blue print" started with the word insight. I needed to understand why I acted the way I did when I committed my crimes. I needed to learn who I am, and who I had become. My ultimate goal was to reform myself.

The lifer class revealed to me some ways to resolve my issues, overcome my triggers and confront my defects. I learned to face past issues, and new coping skills. I learned how to make amends to others and myself. The weekly addendum encouraged me to do self-inventory, to plan strategic goals and importance of daily reflection. These techniques helped me to mature and nourish my personal healing. I have learned to accept challenges and to survive my challenges in a healthy way.

The Victim Sensitivity class helped me become aware of my

need for emotional competence. I came to realize that I had emotions and feelings hinder my life – since I was very young. Just realizing this really educated me about who I am. My emotions and feelings were my weakness and I needed to learn how to control them. This was huge for me. Now when I am tempted, mindful awareness and critical thinking guide me out of tough spots. I now practice this daily.

I consider myself a victim of the public school system. In the past, I had a lot of resentment for the public school system. I felt that I had got a raw deal because of the poor teaching techniques. However, while the teachers could have been more sympathetic, the trauma of my family life was really a distraction to my education. There were some bad teachers at my school. Some would be rude to me when I raised my hand to ask a question. They would never help me, making me feel dumb. My self-esteem took a lot of hits because of teachers like this. They embarrassed and humiliated me. Eventually I dropped out. It has taken me years to erase the negative feelings I would get in a classroom.

The ABE-I/II helped me get past those negative feelings and those bad experiences. Ms. B. teaches at a slow pace and she helps me understand when I miss something. With Ms. B. I have no problem raising my hand to ask a question. Under her, I have advanced so much. I can even see it: my basic skills, my vocabulary, and my confidence have all risen. She encourages me to get my G.E.D.

Another very positive thing about this facility is the blessings of so many other believers in Christ. My mentor is a white brother, Doug Porter. His bible studies have enlightened my spiritual insight beyond measure. The religious program offers a therapeutic course called Reformers Anonymous. It is a religious alternative to Alcoholics Anonymous, but relies biblical principles instead of the 12 steps. This class has helped me overcome my addictions and some of my sinful habits.

Ms. E, a retired teacher comes in and teaches Christian Peace-Makers every Sunday. This class helps us deal with conflict in a biblical way. I now know I can't fight fleshly temptations with fleshly weapons. I have also learned to go beyond having a "religion" but to strive for a relationship with Jesus Christ, and the Holy Spirit. I read the Bible to see specifically what God wants and how he operates. I am learning to be sensitive to the Holy Spirit and it's inner guidance. All of this has helped me to build my faith and relate to many other people. I respect differences and culture.

I'll never forget the hell of maximum security institutions. I do not miss all of the violence. I don't miss all of the long lockdowns. Sometimes we had to sit in the chow hall for hours dressed only in our shower shoes, boxers – handcuffed while the officers searched our cells. During lock-downs, we were escorted in handcuffs to the shower, or the library. Even in the library, we had to wear handcuffs.

I believe many would like to change, but they don't have the resources to revolutionize themselves. I believe a great percentage of people are products of their environment. The PPF does not ease the punishment, but it does give inmates a chance to rehabilitate themselves. This place has given me the opportunity to rectify my life. Since I have been here, I have obtained nineteen laudatory certificates, five certificates of achievement and won an award through a Men For Honor creative writing contest. But the most important award I have earned, and continue to earn, is the skills needed to be successful when I get out, and to contribute to my family. I want to be a productive member of society. Until my release date, I will continue to discover the best in me, reject activities that have no value and embrace pro-social networking. Blessed are the men on the Progressive Programming Facility!

- Some of the descriptions and circumstances listed were changed, with a focus on the violence, not the actual incident.

Kory Darty (A.K.A. "KD") is the father of fourteen- and sixteen-year-old sons. He was born and raised in Jones County/Laurel, Mississippi. He has also lived in Chicago, Illinois, Apple Valley, Minnesota, and Sacramento, California. This thirty-three year old, African-American enjoys creative writing, exploring history, and fellowshipping with those in his Christian faith.

Despite his consistent claims of innocence for the crimes he was convicted of, he takes full responsibility for contaminating his community with illegal drugs and putting others in harm's way. He has taken advantage of his life sentence by educating himself for the past six years since his arrest, and making amends for his errors; he is very generous and will give his last to help others.

Darty also writes encouraging letters to at-risk youth, and enjoys using his trials as a testimony to prove that hardships can be overcome. Darty's faith in Jesus Christ gives him the ability to see the dry land ahead, while still swimming through life's muddy waters. He sees himself as a true diamond in the rough.

RABBI MENACHEM MENDEL

"The world says, time is money, I say, time is life."

A Helping Hand from the Men for Honor

BY VANTRAE GREGORY

After thirty years of prison, and several denials by the parole board, I was finally granted the promise of release on August 27, 2014. One of the reasons I was found suitable was my involvement with Men For Honor.

The Lifers' Class, instructed by Donald Moss, helped me gain insight into my actions, and the effect my crime had on the victim and his next of kin. One of the Board commissioners gave me credit for the essays I wrote. One of the essays was called, "Removing the Mask." In that essay, I described the false persona that I hid behind, and then revealed the real person without the mask. Donald Moss and Dortell Williams helped me with that project.

"In the Victim's Shoes" was written from the perspective of the victim, describing the depth of harm I caused the victim, from his perspective. The Board was convinced that I really understand the gravity of my errors after they read my essays. Lester Polk also helped sharpen my skills in this type of reflective writing.

The class that helped me the most was New Choices, Different Directions, taught by Donald Green. I have a long history of gang involvement, and this anti-gang class helped me replace my destructive viewpoint, and bad habits with positive, and constructive coping mechanisms.

The Board commissioner praised me for my efforts and rehabilitation, and I thank the Men For Honor for helping me get there.

HAUSA PROVERB

"Lack of knowledge is darker than the night"

The Blessing of the Men for Honor

BY DONALD GREEN

Prior to my incarceration, my lifestyle was counter conducive to society's norms and expectations. I was a gang member, a thug, a drug dealer and womanizer. I used whatever tools I could to progress *my own* society. I used drugs and alcohol to suppress the abuse, neglect, and abandonment I had experienced as a child. To cope with the sick reality of my upbringing, I abused drugs and alcohol until my life became completely unmanageable. I was out of control.

In 1993, at the age of twenty-three, I committed a crime that landed me in prison for life. As I entered prison, my sense of misdirection began to accelerate. I fell into that group they call, "prison's worst." I brought my gang affiliation with me, and the negative atmosphere of prison enhanced my destructive attitude. I never thought that I would have the possibility of freedom again.

In 2001, I started to see transformation. I began to see things from a different perspective. I began to pull away from the gang mentality. I wanted to regain my own individuality. It was difficult to get away, and it came to the point where I knew I had to stand up for myself. I started to disassociate myself from the gang, and that lifestyle more and more, making choices that made me more independent. By 2004, I had finally broken away, leaving behind the counter conducive culture for a more normal lifestyle.

In 2007, I found myself more open to positive programming, and I started to get myself together. I started getting involved in self-help programs and wanting to better myself.

In 2011, I arrived at California State Prison-Los Angeles County. My choices had landed me at the Progressive Programming Facility. I immediately took advantage of some of the different programs. They gave me insight into my life, and the destructive lifestyle I had chosen. One of the programs I got involved with was the Men for Honor. I heard a lot of positive things about Men For Honor, and I wanted to be a part of it.

In 2012, I appeared before the Board of Parole Hearing Commissioners. I was denied parole due to my lack of skills in dealing with my anger and stress.

My drive for self-improvement continued, and I kept attending Men For Honor, and other group therapy. I was still learning new coping skills, and the tools necessary to better myself. Men For Honor classes such as Victim Sensitivity and the Lifer's class took me a long way.

Meanwhile, I had been writing various organizations on the outside more specific to my needs. One of those organizations was Criminals and Gangbangers Anonymous, Inc., in Los Angeles. I wrote them and asked for their curriculum. They responded by sending me all of their pamphlets and their curriculum, including their twelve-steps. I told Dortell

Williams and Demetrius Walton, the chairman and vice-chairman at the time, about it, and they arranged a class schedule for me to teach the materials. We got permission to use the materials under Men For Honor, and we called the class, New Choices, Different Directions. We've been running New Choices in cycles for about two years now.

New Choices helped me a lot as well. This course helped me achieve insight into my own criminal background. I learned a lot from CGA just from studying the material alone, but teaching the course, and hearing feedback from others in my same shoes gave me a wider view of our mentality, and how to overcome it.

On December 18, 2013—the happiest day of my life—I went back before the Board of Parole Hearing Commissioners, and this time I was granted parole. The commissioners noted my growth and maturity. I knew the twelve steps for not only CGA, but also Alcoholics and Narcotics Anonymous, and I had no problem explaining my new coping skills. The commissioners were pleased with my involvement with the Men For Honor, and appreciated my leadership in New Choices.

It has been a pleasure to be a part of Men For Honor, while at the same time being transformed into a man of honor.

My Shawshank Redemption

DORTELL WILLIAMS

Next September will mark my 20th year in jail. It is not an anniversary I'm particularly proud of. I was convicted of murder and hopelessly sentenced to life without the possibility of parole.

When I arrived at the infamous Pelican Bay Prison, I was shocked right out of my criminal-minded circuit of stupidity. The flow of in-house narcotics profits didn't appeal to me anymore. My drug-dealing days had already brought me to terrestrial hell.

Like the majority of prisoners on the yard, I just wanted to do my time as trouble-free as possible. I simply wanted to build on the better part of me, redeem whatever part of me was possible. As the cycle of drug abuse, negative peer pressure, and unfettered rebellion roiled around my years of confinement, I began to long for something better. I wanted to be productive, do something better.

That desire to build on the better part of me swelled, but with little comfort and no outlet. With fervent disillusion, I came to see the California Department of Corrections (CDC) as nothing more than an empty shell. It's a colossal department with two overriding modes of operation: 1) behavior control with a heavy stick as its main prod; and 2) the fostering of survival of the fittest, thus encouraging a cut-throat atmosphere of criminal cronyism. In other words, if you don't join a clique, you could be swallowed up as a loner in the predatory food chain.

Scarce are the rewards for positive behavior, especially for lifers. Still, I managed to remain disciplinary free for fourteen consecutive years (dodging the racism, prison-styled hazing, and violent clique initiations), in spite of the pervasive violence, negativity, and hopelessness.

Ironically, it wasn't until I found myself in trouble (for being too friendly with a nurse), that I was transferred to the state prison in Los Angeles County, host of the Prison Honor Program. Suddenly, my lack of cognitive stimulation and productively was turned on its head. There was such a wide array of self-help opportunities to choose from, I didn't know where to start: yoga, creative writing, critical thinking, painting, and many other classes and activities.

I also experienced a different type of peer pressure. My first day out, I was approached by a succession of other prisoners, echoing the same guidance as the first guy: "We don't bang here; we don't play {prison} politics, racial or any other kind; and we respect everyone, including the guards." That speech has been an indelible part of my daily living for the past sixteen years.

I later learned that the program was initiated in 2000 by other reform-minded prisoners. Prisoners who also had an avid desire for inner growth and change. With staff, peer-instructed classes were allowed, using inherent individual talents to sharpen the masses.

To my amazement, not a single class was racially segregated. Everyone interacts and we've come to understand one another better. On the yard, all races play and exercise together, a freakish sight after years of being programmed the other way. Graffiti is nowhere to be found, replaced instead by colorful, creative murals and other works of art.

Since I've been here, racial riots, work stoppages, and the wide range of other wickedness are all memories of the past. I believe this is the only facility in the states that can make such a positive claim.

The success of the Honor Program cannot be denied. According to a study conducted by prison staff, the Honor Program saved the CDC (and taxpayers) more than $200,000 in its first year alone. Meanwhile, weapons infractions decreased 88 percent, and violence and threatening behavior dropped 85 percent.

In a state that features one of the nation's highest recidivism rates – two thirds if California's offenders return to prison within three years – such tangible evidence of behavioral correction is welcome indeed. The secret to this is that it is a completely volunteer program. To our dismay, our success has earned only partial and consistent support from the institution and past secretaries of the department at headquarters in Sacramento.

Sadly, there is still a school of thought that doesn't believe in incentive-based programs or rehabilitation. For members of this camp, continuation of the failed model is sufficient. They want the stick and nothing but the stick. Unfortunately, the violence, deaths, and costly court interventions don't help them see the light.

My hope is that society sees the light and demands life-changing transformation, rather than simply warehousing misery and making human beings subsist the shadows of the dark ages − only to be released back into a neighborhood near you.

Conclusion

The stories in this book underscore three underlying patterns in California prisons (the Department). For decades prisoners have been deprived of the rehabilitative programs that could help them transform their lives. The institutions that were referred to in this book reveal rampant and consistent pathology, causing harm to the prisoners, and spreading the threat to society by failing to rehabilitate its wards.

This book clearly exhibits that prisons are not "cushy" motels, but are dangerous, mismanaged and criminogenic venues that are not only extremely uncomfortable, but inhumane.

The idleness, racism, and other maladaptive behavior that seem part and parcel of the culture of California prisons is winked at by guards and implicitly encouraged by the Department. This malfeasance coupled with the lack of rehabilitative programs offers some understanding and reason for prisoner rebellion and violence.

Given the nearly two decades of contrasting success that the

Honor Yard/Progressive Programming Facility has enjoyed, one could conclude with near certainty that prisoners can commit to personal change if offered consistent programs to help them do so. Indeed, it was the prisoners of the PPF who initiated and designed the program.

Since 2000, the Honor Yard/PPF has never suffered a racial riot, has maintained a consistently lower rate of violence, and prides itself on a culture of camaraderie and collective rehabilitation. The PPF demonstrates that prisoners want rehabilitative programs and will sincerely utilize them if only given the opportunity.

East Oakland Times

The East Oakland Times, LLC (EOT) is a multi-media publication based in the San Francisco Bay Area. Founded by chief editor, Tio MacDonald, EOT has at its core three principles: the principle of the dignity of life, the principle of liberty, and the principle of tolerance. EOT supports the flourishing of civilization through the peace found by honoring these three stated principles.

Current Projects Include:

- Publishing of the My Crime Series: Crime Biographies Written by Inmates, on Inmates.
- The Publication of Original Inmate Books
- Podcasts from California's Condemned Row
- Print Publication for Free Distribution on the Streets of East Oakland
- Indigent Street Vendor Sales Platform in Oakland, CA

Please review Striving for Redemption on Amazon. Reviews are the best way to let others know of the good work being done on the PPF yard.

For more information on the East Oakland Times search for Tio MacDonald on Amazon.com, visit crimebios.com, or navigate to eastoaklandtimes.com

Striving for Redemption can be purchased in bulk (5 books or more) at deep discount prices by contacting the East Oakland Times.

Be positive! Be and stay blessed!
Do good! Love your neighbor and self!

Tio MacDonald
East Oakland Times
Chief Editor

Made in the USA
Las Vegas, NV
25 March 2022

46317143R00108